Stoicism for Beginners

An Empowering Introduction to Stoic Philosophy, Daily Meditations and a Guide to the Art of Joy, Happiness, Positivity, Stress and Life — Be Happy, Stop Anxiety and Beat Depression!

Tobias Entwistle

All Copyrights Reserved.

TABLE OF CONTENTS

INTRODUCTION 1

CHAPTER ONE : STOICISM: HISTORY AND PHILOSOPHY 4

CHAPTER TWO : STOICISM: IN THE MODERN WORLD 11

CHAPTER THREE : KNOW THYSELF 19

CHAPTER FOUR : THE POWER OF MEDITATION 28

CHAPTER FIVE : CHOOSING VIRTUE AHEAD OF IMMORALITY 35

CHAPTER SIX : ELIMINATING EMOTIONS 44

CHAPTER SEVEN : BEING LOGICAL AT ALL TIMES ... 52

CHAPTER EIGHT : LIVING A STRESS-FREE LIFE 57

CHAPTER NINE : BEATING DEPRESSION WITH STOICISM 64

CHAPTER TEN : BEING CALM AMIDST ADVERSITIES 72

CHAPTER ELEVEN : INDIFFERENCE: UNVEILING THE GOODNESS IN YOU 82

CHAPTER TWELVE : A PINCH OF STOICISM IN OUR DAILY LIVES 89

CHAPTER THIRTEEN : STOICISM: A PATHWAY TO JOY, HAPPINESS, AND POSITIVITY 95

CHAPTER FOURTEEN : AFTER THE STORM, COMES

PEACE 101

CHAPTER FIFTEEN : A NEW DAWN! 110

CONCLUSION 123

Introduction

When we hear the word "stoicism," "stoics," or even "stolidity," one thing keeps ringing in our head - indifference! Indifference to pain, indifference to pleasure, indifference to our sense of reasoning, and indifference to our raging emotions. Nevertheless, stoicism goes way beyond just Indifference. It encapsulates our very existence.

It is important to know that stoicism as a philosophy started more than a thousand years ago. As a matter of fact, early stoicism dates back to the days of the old Athens, in the Greek setting. Zeno was the father of early stoicism with many scholars and thinkers doting on his philosophy, even after his death.

Many centuries later, the term stoicism became synonymous with thinkers of antiquities such as Kant, Montaigne, Deleuze, and Nietzsche. According to these scholars, the world and humans are two connected but distinct components which should work hand in hand for a better cosmos.

They further believe that the world is materially and secularly inclined with humans playing a role in this formation, especially as a rational animal. However, the rise and introduction of the Modern Stoics saw the regression of the views, tenets, and beliefs of the early Stoics as it contradicts with the true nature and set up of the modern world.

This gave birth to the paradigm shift in some of the core values of the principles of Stoicism. Modern day Stoicism now focus on the acknowledgment of facts ahead of nature, elimination of violent emotions toward much better reasoning, and upholding virtue as the only gateways towards being happy.

In other words, a clear mind devoid of emotions is a perfect mind. Be that as it may, what this book seeks to do is familiarize and enlighten you on the concepts of Stoicism. It also seeks to take you through a stress-free journey of being a better version of what you were yesterday.

A lot of people have made their mistakes from making what could have been a simple problem into a cumbersome one. If only they had added a little bit of logic and emotionless attitude, the problem would have been dealt with accordingly. But most times, we tend to let our emotions take total control of us, thereby making decisions that will leave us unhappy in the end.

This book will equip you with the right mindset toward making a better judgment, even in the face of adversity. It will enlighten you on how to beat depression and anxiety without even trying. Read through the chapters with rapt attention, and I can assure you you'll come out stronger, better, and wiser in making decisions that influence your life.

We all deserve to be happy. We all deserve to lead a good life. Clear your mind and allow us to take you through this breathtaking experience. Happy reading!

Chapter One

Stoicism: History and Philosophy

The old Greek setting has been quite popular for its wonderful and soul-captivating theories, principles, and philosophies, which are still very vital in today's world. Even after these theories, principles, and philosophies had been conceived for over thousands of years, they still remain vital and relevant in today's world, thereby forming the roots of all modern work.

For instance, the great Greek scholars of antiquities like Socrates, Aristotle, and Plato have become tenets and foundations which had given birth to lots of modern works out there. Notwithstanding, it is important to know that philosophies during the old Greek setting feature every aspect and corner of the world in general.

From war to love, nature, science, geography, biology, and so much more. With that being said, our focus will be on one of Greek finest philosophies - Stoicism.

Ancient Stoicism was first started as a movement in the late 300 BCE by the great Zeno of Citium before it gradually graduated into a school of thought. As a movement, the believers of this early philosophy met at the popular "Painter Stao," which is located at the market place of Greece's most populous city, Athens. Little wonder why the school of thought got its name "Stoic."

Unlike the already well-established school of Plato (Academy), Aristotle's school (Lyceum), and the Epicurus school (Garden), which was gaining momentum during that period, Zeno's Stoic movement was just beginning to establish itself as an upcoming, new school of thought. They never had the opportunity and facilities these other schools had.

As a matter of fact, they only met at various public spots situated in the city of Athens. It is important to know that Stoicism started gaining much popularity only after the death of its founder, Zeno of Citium. Little by little, Zeno's student, Cleanthes, carried on with the propagation of his teacher's work.

People of Athens now begin to infuse and inculcate Stoicism in their daily life, thereby giving the school of thought a heavy boost throughout the city.

Stoicism and the Roman Empire

Over the course of time, Rome rose to become the center of power and politics during the first century BCE. Romans had studied the Stoic philosophy and deemed it perfect for their fast-growing nation. The ideologies and principles of Zeno's school of thought became the guiding force toward leading the glorious Rome.

This was evident in the summaries Cicero introduced to the Latin-speaking world on the importance of mastering Stoicism. Afterward, there was a large acceptance and reception of Stoicism all over Rome, and especially in other cities of the world, such as Seneca, Lucan, Perseus, Musonius, Rufus, and Epictetus.

Romans now saw life from a whole new perspective, unlike what the other schools had posited. Stoicism taught them rationality. Stoicism taught them accountability for their actions. Stoicism taught them the real meaning of life. It taught them what was right and wrong.

To this effect, Stoicism encapsulates different core theories ranging from ethics, epistemology, and ontology. It opens up your mind to see the true nature of the world. Nevertheless, before Zeno became inspired by this philosophy, there were chunks of previous philosophies that had laid emphasis on this line of thoughts.

So the question remains, what makes Stoicism stands out? The difference is very clear in the central tenets and focus of the Stoic philosophical system. The Stoics posit that the world is materially inclined. It is driven by a material force which is created by a supernatural being.

It also argued that for us to be eternally happy, we must uphold virtue and morality alone. Material benefits are totally irrelevant in attaining genuine happiness. Furthermore, our emotions shouldn't guide our judgments and deductions. In fact, they are merely a product of our irrationality and should be eliminated.

Stoicism thereby encourages you to be rational, devoid of emotions, and indifferent to events, phenomena, and activities revolving around you. The principle of Stoicism had painted its school of thought around a picture of a perfect man who would only attain true happiness even in the face of torture by upholding morality and virtue, thereby becoming highly rational, emotionless, and indifferent.

Stoicism later grew in followers over time. The loss of major traditional text which points to the early principles of the school of thought led to its high regression in the third century BCE. However, the philosophy started gaining grounds as modern philosophers started building on the origin of the school.

The Cicero Summary which was written in Latin, fragments of the "Painted Stao" gathering written by early authors, and other early works gave credence to the school's postulations. This further boosted their influence in the sixteenth and seventeenth century.

Key Concept of the Philosophy

1. Virtue and Morality: Early Stoics believed that there was more to life than just reckless living. The only way to attain real happiness is via upholding virtue and morality. While many of the schools in the old Greek setting contradict this concept, Stoics believe these two concepts are what we need to live a meaningful life.

They believe morality and virtue define courage, good character, justice, and good traits. Not many people possess these kind of outstanding qualities. Thus, mastering and studying the philosophy of Stoicism is the only way one can truly understand the principles.

To this effect, it is pertinent to know that in order to live a stress-free life, one must not only study the principles of Stoicism academically but also infuse them into our way of life practically.

Stoics also posit that all humans have the tendency and free will to choose from what is right and what is wrong. They have the tendency to follow the path of morality or virtue and not immorality or evil. In other words, we are accountable for every one of our actions, either good or bad.

2. Emotions: According to Stoics, anyone who can successfully devoid themselves of emotions when making decisions, irrespective of the circumstances, would eventually live a fulfilled life. In other words, he who can eliminate or separate himself from emotions at all times is a complete Stoic.

With that being said, the idea of emotions is not entirely evil to the Stoics. This will be further explained in the next chapter of this book. To this effect, we shouldn't let this be the drive behind our decision making. If we let our emotions take the better part of us, we might end up not making a very smart move.

Thus, a rational way of making a decision is the best way we can follow in coming up with logical solutions to our problems. The sweet feeling that comes with making the right decision is the only true and appropriate emotion we should feel.

So don't get it twisted, Stoics are actually in support of emotions. Emotions are feelings we can't do without. But they should be sidelined and differentiated from the important aspects of human existence (decision making, judgments, living a good life, and maintaining nature).

3.   Harmonic Co-existence: This is one great concept about Stoicism. Irrespective of our principles, ideologies, and way of life, we shouldn't cease to co-exist in peace and harmony. This can only be achieved via our strive toward a logical existence. According to the words of Marcus Aurelius in his Meditations,

"We were born for cooperation, like feet, like hands, like eyelids, like the rows of upper and lower teeth. So to work in opposition to one another is against nature: and anger or rejection is opposition."

Stoicism focuses on the connection between man and nature. They both are a part of the whole. Thus, they should work together in harmony. In other words, living a careful and stress-free life, putting nature first, and maintaining our environment.

Want to be a Stoic? It's very simple! All you need to do is to master the principles and tenets. Stoicism as a philosophy has helped a lot of people become truly happy. It has helped rise nations and organizations. Practice Stoicism every day of your life and watch yourself move from leading a normal life to living a happy life. However, the face of Stoicism changed in the new world as there is a paradigm shift in its concepts and ideas.

This and more is what we will discuss in the next chapter. You wouldn't want to miss it.

Chapter Two

Stoicism: In the Modern World

The late 20th century and the early 21st century ushered in the beginning of a new era of Stoicism. The world today has taken a whole new dimension with the presence of many diverse schools of thought in stiff competition with the Stoic philosophy. Nevertheless, Stoicism in the modern world covers the efforts, infusion, and inculcation of Stoic beliefs with the present state of nature.

Therefore, it is important to note that the early tenets of this school cannot be originally applied without tweaking and making the necessary adjustments to suit the current state of the world.

Like we know, the world itself entails changing phases and events. A lot has changed from the first century to the present century. Philosophies have evolved, new inventions are pioneered, and ideas are refurbished. To this effect, old Stoicism can also be said to have passed through the process of reformation and transformation, so as to blend in with the present world.

These blended ideas and movement are what is called Modern Stoicism. Modern Stoicism regained quite a bit of recognition all over the world in

November 2012 after the successful event of the First Annual Stoic Week which took place at Exeter University in England. According to statistics, the blogs got numerous hits, over 150 people signed up to the Stoic Week page every week, and notable newspapers like the Guardian and the Independent also graced pages of their newspapers with articles on the event.

Ever since then, the idea of living like a Stoic has been well received, especially with the way people now live their lives with less importance. They now begin to see Stoicism in a different light as it enlightens them on how to really live one's life with absolute contentment.

Virtue and morality theme the arguments of all Modern Stoics. For example, the notable and scholarly works of Alasdair MacIntyre and Philippa Foot have laid emphasis on the need for virtue and morality, which in turn signals the presence of Stoicism. Even in the early Stoic principles, virtue and morality championed their arguments.

One man all Modern Stoics can claim to have drawn their ideas and formed their roots from is none other than Lawrence Becker. In Becker's major Stoicism work named "A New Stoicism", which was published in 1997, he writes,

"It is interesting to try to imagine what might have happened if Stoicism had had a continuous twenty-three hundred year history; if Stoics had had to confront Bacon and Descartes, Newton and Locke, Hobbes and Bentham, Hume and Kant, Darwin and Marx."

Following the above quote of Lawrence Becker, you would agree with me that the early tenets, beliefs, and principles had to be brushed up so as to fit the present statuesque. However, brushing up doesn't necessarily mean that the philosophy has lost its core values. As a matter of fact, it still remains the same, but with a much better approach and view of the world.

Modern Stoic Philosophy

There has been a divide in the philosophical beliefs of Modern Stoicism. Logic, Physics, and Ethics are the three notable elements that make up Ancient Stoic beliefs. However, a lot of Modern Stoic scholars have argued that the latter (Ethics) alone holds up the tenets of Stoicism with Logic and Physics adding little or no value to the already laid principles.

In the same vein, other Modern Stoic scholars believe this notion is outright wrong. In fact, the old Stoics innovated the tenets and beliefs of Stoicism around these three topoi (core areas); Physics, Logic, and Ethics, for a reason.

Physics encapsulates other core areas such as science, theology, and metaphysics. These areas help us gain a better understanding of the modern world as a material cosmos. Ethics, on the other hand, goes way beyond what is right and what is wrong. It entails how to lead a good life, how to be genuinely happy, and so much more.

Logic covers more ground than just the formal logic outlook other scholars tend to attach to it. It goes way beyond that. It touches informal logic down to rhetoric, psychology, and cognitive science.

Stoicism all points to deriving true happiness from living a good life. How about making rational and logical conclusions and decisions to lead a good life? How about understanding nature, so as to be able to make good and rational decisions? You can see they are all connected, right? Ethics go hand in hand with Logic and Physics in order to master Stoicism.

Modern Stoicism as a Movement

The Modern Stoicism movement is a global phenomenon. Nevertheless, the world is globally in sync, with ICT holding the strong chain that binds every part of it together. When we say ICT, we are referring to social media and online activities. To this effect, the propagation of Modern Stoicism has relied heavily on the use of mass media and online platforms.

The First Annual Stoic Week held at Exeter University in England gave popularity to the movement as it was heavily broadcasted online, in blogs, and in newspapers. In 1996, another important online platform was created (The New Stao) and has been able to reach millions of people over the last two decades.

Podcasts also gave credence to the movement. The Sunday Stoic and The Practical Stoic podcasts are examples of the many podcasts that sprung up, gaining interests from people from all over the world.

Internet had no doubt provided Stoics with a brand new way to preach their gospel to anyone that cared to listen. From blogs to newspapers, podcasts, social media (Facebook, Twitter, etc.), and any other internet gateways.

Aside from the internet, there has been an increase in the number of meet-ups, conventions, events, and workshops in places like Helsinki, Denver, London, San Francisco, Warsaw, Australia, Manchester, Milwaukee, Dublin, and many more.

Modern stoics are synonymous with beliefs that there should be a change in the society as regards economic slump, gender discrimination, immortality and evil, environmental treatment, material consumption, reckless living, accountability for our decisions and actions taken, and so much more.

Notable Key Concepts

1. Virtue, Agency, and Happiness: Modern Stoics like Lawrence Becker believe that virtue, agency, and happiness go hand in hand. In other words, the call for virtue can only be perfected through the right organization of agencies, which in turn would lead to true happiness.

One who has a great amount of control and stability over his or herself is bound to be happy in the long run - even if not immediately. The agency in this view is understood to be our being or self. If we uphold the necessary virtues and exert them on our decisions and judgments, we will surely end up being happier than we have ever been.

2. Nature: Even the Ancient Stoics believed in the maintenance of nature. Thus, in order to lead a life of virtue and be truly happy, nature must be maintained and cherished. They also posited that nature is inherently good and the purpose of its creation is toward a good end.

Therefore, if we follow nature, we will surely end up being good. Nevertheless, the Ancient Stoics' view of nature cannot be applied or can be very difficult in its application to the modern world, especially with the way everything is being configured by science and technology.

Now, the following of nature can be quite wrong, especially with the rate of genocide, atrocities, and evil the modern world is characterized by. If this old Stoic belief is followed, one might be completely out of bounds. Thus, seeing nature as inherently good doesn't hold much substance.

Many Modern Stoics like Lawrence Becker have given their opinions on this concept of "following nature." According to their assumption, Stoicism would have been perfect without the "following nature" concept. But the bad news is that the concept had been synonymous with Stoicism for far too long. Thus, eliminating this concept would mean eliminating an important part of Stoicism.

To this effect, a reinterpretation of the concept became the next best thing to do by this group of Modern Stoics. They believed that instead of following nature blindly like the traditional Stoics, facts about nature should be followed instead. Now the question remains, what does "following facts" mean?

Simply put, following facts means getting the necessary facts about events, phenomena, and circumstances that surround us before making conclusions and judgments. That way, we will end up achieving true happiness.

3. Ascetic and Renunciation: Stoicism tenets focus on the indifference to both the pains and pleasures of our lives. According to early Stoics, attaining this indifference would make you a complete Stoic. In other words, differentiating your emotions from your reasoning and judgment is key.

However, there is no generally acceptable unit used in measuring ascetic elements oer defining the pleasures and pains of life. Nevertheless, we shouldn't mistake Stoicism for Asceticism. They are both completely different things.

First of all, Stoicism believes true happiness can only be attained when people reach eudemonia - and not from the ordinary material pleasures life would offer you. A stoic is not a monk. Stoicism goes beyond living an ascetic life. As a matter of fact, Stoicism entails accepting nature along with its goodness, lushness, diversity, and sensuality.

Little wonder why lots of people today now see the true meaning of existence. It goes beyond getting that esteemed college degree. It goes beyond having a perfect family. It also goes beyond getting a six-figure monthly salary. Being truly happy while fulfilling the true meaning of life is what our consequent chapters will discuss. But before then, one really needs to understand oneself in order to know which steps to take toward being a true Stoic.

Now, the question remains, how well do you know yourself? Want to find out? Then flip the page over.

Chapter Three

Know Thyself

One of the greatest and shortest quotes ever said by an ancient Greek philosopher (Socrates) is "Know Thyself." These can be said to be the words of a dying man before facing persecution by his Greek lords and authorities. With these simple words, he has challenged even the dumbest of us into checking ourselves to see if we truly know our own selves.

Today, knowing ourselves is the first step one must take before reformation, transformation, and refurbishment. Sometimes, we might have made decisions that do not favor us in the long run. We obviously won't know this at first because our sense of reasoning or judgment might have been influenced by emotions.

But after some time, we start seeing things clearly. Questions now begin to run through our minds. Questions like: Are we making the best decisions for ourselves? Is this truly what we deserve? What would we have done if given a second chance?

Knowing oneself is what pushed the Zeno of Citium into giving birth to this philosophy in the first place. A brief study into his life would enlighten you on the importance of knowing oneself and knowing what is right from what is wrong In order to live a glorious and happy life.

Zeno of Citium was a sailing merchant who had spent more than half of his life inside the confines of a ship. He had derived joy in making ends meet with this line of trade and it was working very well for him. Now, imagine how one would have easily thought of a sailing merchant transforming into one of the founders of the Greek school of thoughts. Quite crazy, right?

Well, it's pretty easy. Some events and circumstances in life end up unlocking a part of us we never knew existed, making us see life in a clearer view. This same thing happened to Zeno of Citium. But in his case, an unforgettable experience. A shipwreck changed the next chapters of his life.

This change of events in his life opened up a new path he sought out. It made him go through the sober reflection phase, which shone lights on a certain aspect of his life that he had neglected. This made him understand himself even better. The shipwreck that almost claimed his life spurred up something in him – the hope and desire to lead a good and happy life.

Now let's ask ourselves this question: Has any event, circumstance, or happening revolving around us spurred up the real us? It is important to know that after Zeno of Citium knew himself better, things changed for him. A new light shone on a new path which he followed. Only then, he became really happy, wise, and articulate.

He knew the solution to the unhappiness of people around him, the solution to the stressful life people around him led, the solution to the atrocities and evil people around him portrayed. He also knew sentiments and emotions do more harm than good. They will never get anybody anywhere. Thus, he founded Stoicism.

Aside Zeno of Citium, a lot of other scholars of this school of thought have also made their mark and contribution towards the development of the philosophy. They have also followed the philosophy of knowing oneself. There is no greater joy than knowing exactly what you want and how to go about achieving it.

Don't get it twisted, people might not buy your idea or even like what you want to begin with. They may criticize and oppose you any opportunity they get. You won't let that deter you from achieving your aims, will you? Your happiness should definitely matter ahead of what others feel or think about your opinion.

Bill Gates didn't get where he is now as a result of letting people's opinions get to him. As a matter of fact, Bill Gates dropped out of college after knowing what he wanted at that particular time. When others were busy bagging their degrees, he was busy turning himself into a better version of what he was. He was busy doing what made him happy.

Don't get me wrong - getting a degree is great, if not superb. But knowing yourself, knowing what you want, and aiming for those things is what will bring you complete happiness. Everyone has his or her own drive. Know yours and happiness would surely be yours.

Now, imagine if Bill Gates had decided not to follow his dreams, his wants, and his path, would he have been truly happy? The answer is no. I'm sure no one would even be able to picture Bill Gates without Microsoft.

It is important to know that knowing oneself is the first step toward being a Stoic. Knowing oneself points to only one thing - coming to terms with being extremely happy by following the dictations of your mind, your desires, your dreams, and your aspirations. These wants end up contributing to the further development of humanity, which is one of the guiding principles of being a Stoic.

A Stoic upholds and maintains the relationship between man and nature. And in order for you to achieve these dreams and goals, your decisions and judgments must be devoid of emotions and sentiments. These and more are the core attributes of a true Stoic.

Just like Zeno of Citium, knowing oneself to be a

Stoic is just one step. Familiarizing yourself with the philosophy and practicing it is another step entirely. After the shipwreck which opened a new path for Zeno of Citium, he developed an urge to learn about Greek philosophies, therefore visiting famous books stores in Athens as he embarked on his quest to quench his thirst for knowledge.

He knew he had to seek out books and records of other notable Greek philosophers, so as to get a grip on the basics of all Greek philosophies. Therefore, through your research and findings on Stoicism, I'm sure you will be able to understand yourself even better. Additionally, being a true Stoic comes with being accountable for your decisions and actions.

Before setting out your plans, be sure to be accountable for every action taken. Stoicism will give definition to your life. Instead of living a life of immorality, Stoicism wikk teach you virtue, compassion, humility, and moderation.

Steps to Knowing Oneself

1. Connect to Your Inner Self: This is the first step to knowing yourself. Reaching your inner chakra can be accomplished a lot of ways. Some people may prefer yoga, while others just want to have a nice cool, quiet place where they can think. Be that as it may, we would recommend you record or write down your every thought.

Keep a journal, if possible so that all your thoughts are compiled in a safe place. In the long run, it would surely serve you well as you would be able to revise and go back to the ideas, dreams, and aspirations written or recorded.

Writing in a journal while connecting to your inner self helps you focus and keep your mind afloat from different thoughts and stress. In the end, you will be able to understand, comprehend, and know yourself even better. Connecting to your inner self will clarify your thoughts. It will separate that which is important from which is irrelevant.

2. Sober Reflection: Sometimes, when we end up making a wrong move or decision, sober reflection becomes the next best thing to do. Go back to the point where it all began. Then imagine what you would do if the situation presented itself again.

Sober Reflection can only take effect when you retire in solitude. Keep yourself in a quiet place devoid of noise of any kind. That will help you focus on replaying your life over and over again. Rest assured, this process will only make you a better version of yourself.

Your relationship will improve with everyone around you. Sober Reflection sheds light on the path to becoming a better person. It gives you the opportunity to know yourself even better.

3. Set Standards: Our core beliefs, principles, and standards are what differentiate us from everybody else. It's what differentiates nations, organizations, and entities. So, therefore, know your standards, so as to set standards that are convenient to you alone. Keep and stick to them no matter what.

Knowing yourself comes with setting your life according to your own terms and standards. These standards ensure that you don't live your life recklessly. As a matter of fact, they are the guiding mechanisms that check our decisions, actions, reactions, and judgments in ensuring we don't live outside our own convenience.

4. Take Responsibility for Your Actions: Knowing yourself toward living a happy life comes with honesty and responsibility. No matter what, always be accountable for your actions - no matter how shallow or irrational they may be. Your life is in your hands, thus you should know how to tell what is right from what is wrong.

Don't forget you have a journal that consists of all your strengths and weaknesses. Try to visit this journal from time to time. Know what is right from what is wrong, know your strengths from your weaknesses, and focus on what will make you a better version of yourself.

5. Know What Motivates You: Finding our life purposes can be easier than we had imagined. Motivation differs from person to person. Like the saying goes, "One man's meat is another man's poison." So ask yourself, what motivates you? What do you think can spur up inspiration in you?

6. Weigh Your Relationships: Check your circle. How well do you support one another? How well does your circle help project your true self? These are questions we should ask ourselves when weighing our circle. A relationship is meant to help us to be our very best.

If your circle doesn't include or possess this attribute, then we suggest you start changing it. Most times, the right relationships show us where our problems lie. They nurture and nourish us into becoming our true selves. Thus, we need to handle our relationships with great importance. Those in our world end up becoming the mirrors that reflect our true selves.

Knowing thyself is the key to real happiness. It is the first step to take in preparing your mind. What do you really think you are capable of holding? Are you really willing to let go of your emotions? Is this really what you want? These and more are the questions we should ask ourselves.

No one can tell us about ourselves the way we understand it. Know your self and what you want first - and the best way of doing that is to go into meditation. Want to know how? Then read through our next chapter, as we will walk you through the conversation on how meditation will bring out the real you as well as pave the way for more happiness in your life.

Chapter Four

The Power of Meditation

One of the powerhouses of this school of thought, Marcus Aurelius, has given a lot of insight on the positive effect of meditation toward achieving true happiness. According to his words in his popular book *Meditation*,

"The art of true living in this world is more like a wrestler's, than a dancer's practice. For in this they both agree, to teach a man whatsoever falls upon him, that he may be ready for it, and that nothing may cast him down."

It is important to know that Marcus Aurelius was the Roman Emperor between 161 to 180 AD, and during this period, Rome faced a lot of adversities and hardships. As a Stoic philosopher, meditation became the only way he could reflect on his life. Meditation also became the only way he could seek solutions to the current events disturbing Rome.

As portrayed in the popular movie *Gladiator*, Marcus Aurelius was presented as a good man who faced lots of tribulations and atrocities: Invasion from the borders, internal revolt and coup, and so much more. This is very correct. However, the movie's final scene, showing Marcus Aurelius son murder him is not correct. In reality, Marcus died of smallpox.

Imagine you are a young, open-minded, outright good fellow with lots of betrayers in your circle, who would you trust? What would you do? This is the exact situation Marcus Aurelius faced in his reign as the Emperor of Rome.

He had no one to turn to, so he turned to himself. Meditation gave him a clear head. It helped him continue to stay on the path of righteousness, irrespective of the situations, circumstances, and events revolving around him. That is the power meditation holds.

Be like Marcus Aurelius. Whenever you are faced with issues that may cause an obstacle to your Stoic beliefs and principles, go into that meditation Marcus did, and make sure you come out as a better version of what you were before. Nothing should stop you from reaching your dreams - and in the end, becoming very happy.

You can also write down your meditations just like Marcus Aurelius. These written meditations of Marcus Aurelius have contributed to the Modern Stoic sources of the philosophy. His meditations have helped lay the foundations of Modern Stoicism. The meditation is divided into 12 books and each represents a specific period of time in the life of Marcus Aurelius.

Many Modern scholars believe that Marcus Aurelius meditation was written solely for his own benefit. However, it remains the foundation that holds the Stoic philosophy together. It is simple to comprehend, highly conversational, and easy to read by just anybody.

Meditation and happiness can be said to be two sides of the same coin. The practice goes a long way in moving us from being stressed to being serene. One way or another, it works like magic. Sometimes, we just end up being stressed out. We might even reach a point where giving up would seem like the only option left for us to choose. But have we tried meditation? Just a few minutes of meditation can wash away hours of stress and anxiety.

What meditation does is to refocus your energy into something positive. That way, your energy will be redirected and you will be filled with positivity afterward. According to research, people feel happier after a few minutes of meditation.

As a matter of fact, they stand more upright. They begin to smile more often. They also start accepting themselves with joy concerning how they look, how they sound, how they walk, how they keep their relationships, and even how they coexist with everyone around them.

Marcus Aurelius hit an iceberg of tribulations during his reign as the Roman Emperor. Yet, he was determined to be happy and live a good life. Thus, he started meditating. The happiness that comes out of meditation is real. It lasts longer because of the redirected energy in us.

Don't get it twisted, other happiness boosters like going on vacation, going on a shopping spree, going to a mind-blowing event, spending time with family, and so much more are also great. But the question is - how long do they really last? They wear off as fast as you can imagine, leaving you with the same awful feelings you'd felt before, over and over again.

Additionally, meditation comes quite cheap. You can be in the confines of your room and still meditate. It will only take a few minutes or even hours of your time, depending on the amount of free time you on your hands. We would like you to consider it as the price you'd get to pay for keeping the glow it will give to your face afterward.

There is no measure of the amount of happiness meditation will offer you. Even in the midst of atrocities and tribulations, it kept Marcus Aurelius really happy. Instead of breaking down, it helped him grow stronger in his Stoic beliefs and principles. With meditation, there are no expectations you won't be able to meet, no hurdle you won't be able to cross over, and no obstacle you will not be able to overcome.

Nevertheless, some people are just naturally happy,

irrespective of where life places them. But this population is very small in today's world as a majority of us are always grumpy, sad, and unhappy. This is not because we don't have or possess the material benefits to bring us temporary happiness, but because we lack what it takes to be genuinely happy.

Like we said in the previous chapters, no one is a true Stoic until he or she reaches the stage of eudemonia. How can we reach this stage? It's pretty simple. Meditation is one of the gateways to reaching Eudemonia. Little wonder why meditation is now taken seriously by people in the 21st century.

As a matter of fact, a major Information Technology company in Detroit, Michigan made their employees go through a 60 minutes meditation session within the span of seven weeks - and the result was simply overwhelming. There was an immense increase in the focus, emotions, and energy of the employees toward work.

This, in turn, increases the output (i.e. Mindfulness, zeal toward work, decreased illness, increased friendliness, relaxed the tensed working atmosphere, etc.). This is the power of meditation. It makes your goals and purposes in life become much clearer while giving you a clear mind to pursue those goals into reality.

How to Meditate

Meditation is not as hard as people or the media advertises it to be. Notwithstanding, it goes beyond just sitting on a mat wearing fancy pants. It involves concentration. It involves reaching your inner self.

To begin with, finding the perfect place for meditation is vital. You just can't go out there and spread your mat all in the name of meditation. What if it's noisy? What if it's a busy environment? What if it's cold? What if it's hot? These are the questions we should ask ourselves. Get a nice, quiet, comfortable environment or space.

After getting the perfect spot, spread your meditation mat, or cushion as the case may be, and sit or lie comfortably. Be sure to be very comfortable in your sitting style or lying techniques. We wouldn't want a situation where our back, thighs, or even joints might end up hurting at the end of our meditation.

Then closing our eyes and refocusing our mind is the next thing to do. This should force out any negative thoughts that have been going through our minds so as to give us a clear mind in the end. One mistake people make is to start controlling their breathing. This is a mistake. Instead, breathe naturally. Do not breathe heavily, but instead lightly.

Focus on your breathing pace. It is very important

to maintain your concentration. And in any case, when your mind wanders off, let your breathing draw you back to your meditation. If you feel numb or tired, you can change your sitting or lying postures - but make sure to maintain concentration.

Do this for as long as you can and you will definitely feel refreshed and renewed. Meditation provides answers to questions we can't seem to find answers to, especially when the outside world is not helping. Tired of seeking advice from people who are not even worth a listening ear? Then look inward and concentrate on your inner citadel with meditation. The answers you need are right there.

But the question remains, do you have the courage to follow it? Read on to the next chapter as we enlighten you on one of Stoics' key principles - Virtue.

Chapter Five

Choosing Virtue Ahead of Immorality

Following what we have discussed in the previous chapters, we have come to understand that one of the key concepts of Stoicism is Virtue and Morality. Stoicism, according to its proponents, scholars, and practitioners, believes that true happiness can be achieved by choosing virtue and morality over sin, reckless living, and immorality. In order words, choosing good over evil in our daily life is the only way a person can achieve true happiness

But rest assured, virtue is part of what we exude almost every day of our lives. Being good to your next door neighbor is a virtue. Helping an old woman cross a busy road is a virtue. As a matter of fact, anything good is a virtue. Thus, the Stoics didn't go wrong when they laid emphasis on being good.

What is Virtue?

Virtue is defined by Stoics as the knowledge of living life the best way - a way that revolves around all aspects of life including personal and business. Furthermore, virtue is a disposition or state where one is considered to be praiseworthy or good. There are four main cardinals that define this state called virtue. It is safe to say these four cardinals are used to analyze the concept of virtue.

The Four Cardinals of Virtue

The four cardinals of virtue are considered as a means of creating an outline to the main events, experiences, and expertise surrounding human life. Stoic theorists believe that the successful combination and infusion of these four cardinals into our existence is the only way one can live a virtuous and fulfilled life.

If one possesses these four characters, according to Stoicism, the person is referred to as a good and a virtuous person. These four cardinals of virtue are as follows:

1. **Wisdom (Sophia):** Wisdom, or Sophia as referred to in the Greek language, has to do with knowledge and understanding. It is insight, common sense, experience, prudence, and knowledge. This cardinal of virtue is the most general and most important of all the four cardinals. Wisdom here has to do with grasping of knowledge of the good, the bad and the indifferent in life and humanity.

It goes further to emphasize understanding the core value of things and rationally acting upon these values. In other words, wisdom is knowing how to act and understanding what to do in a different situation.

To Stoics, wisdom means understanding and knowing the nature of good. That is, understanding wisdom and living accordingly is true good and a path to happiness. Early Stoic proponents and scholars already laid a firm background to the explanation of wisdom or prudence.

Marcus explained wisdom as the ability to respond to things "in accord with value".

According to Diogenes Laertius, who referred to Chrysippus and others, wisdom or prudence is classified into good counsel (euboulia) and understanding (sunesis).

Stobaeus also said that early Stoics explained wisdom to be the knowing of good and bad, understanding indifference, and knowing the "appropriate action" to take in every situation. It is clear that the Stoics believe that being wise is equal to good.

2.   Courage (Andreia): Courage, or Andreia, according to Stoics is a disposition of the mind that is unmoved by fear. It is self-restraint of the soul in situations that are fearful and terrible. Courage is the ability to face intimidation, uncertainty, pain, danger, and agony head on.

In order words, Stoics explain courage as knowing what to do, how to feel, and how to act when faced with adversity and fear in situations of danger like death and other disasters. Diogenes Laertius refers to the classification of courage into two parts by early proponents, which are determination (apparallaxia) and tension (eutonia).

Stobaeus also refer to courage as knowing and understanding what is terrible, what is not terrible, and what is neither (unmoved). Senaca observed that without some traces of fear, virtue cannot exist, because every single person, no matter how perfect or virtuous, needs a little courage.

With the above definitions and explanations, we can come to the conclusion that courage is endurance guided by wisdom.

3. Self-Control (Sophrosune): This cardinal of virtue has to do with self-control, temperance, and moderation. This virtue focuses on moderating the soul's pleasures and desires and the ability to discipline one's self when facing desires and pleasures. This is a state or disposition which deals with cautiousness or mindfulness. Modern Christianity is said to have gotten the idea of moral conscience from the virtue of moderation.

This virtue can be defined or analyzed as self-discipline or self-control with self-awareness and self-possession. It is our impulse that guides our reactions and intentions on different desires. Moderation as a virtue is directly opposite to the vice wantonness.

Stobaeus explained moderation here as what is to chosen, avoided and neither. Diogenes Laerteus says the early Stoics defined moderation basically as good discipline. They also subdivided this virtue of moderation into propriety (eutaxia) and decorum (kosmistes). In other words, having the rationale to choose the right thing over one's heart;a desire and pleasure is a form of being virtuous.

4. Justice/Morality (dikaiosune): This good virtue is simply the good discipline of the soul with respect and concern to one another. Justice is goodwill to others, kindness, and benevolence. It is the state or disposition where one chooses what is just. This is a situation of choosing a law-abiding path to life and social equality. This is simply obeying the laws already in place.

In Stoicism, justice doesn't only mean being just in the legal sense. It also has to do with being just in the moral sense, not only in our personal dealings but in our dealings with others and humanity in general. In the early years of Stoicism, its scholars and practitioners referred to this virtue as righteousness, but in modern times it is safe to define this virtue as morality. The direct vice to this virtue is being unjust or morally doing wrong by another person.

In order words, justice can be viewed as prudence applied to our actions. Stobaeus defined justice as understanding and the knowledge of distributing fair value to everyone. According to Diogenes Laertius, Stoics subdivided justice into impartiality (isotes) and kindness (eugnomosune).

Immorality

Immorality is equal to a violation of moral laws, moral standards, and moral norms. It is a state or disposition of badness and wickedness. Stoics believe that immorality is the highest form of vice which is the direct opposite of virtue and should be stayed away from in order to achieve full happiness and live a fulfilled life.

Immorality is shunned upon by Stoics, and this philosophy preaches choosing virtue ahead of immorality and sin. The concept of immorality is considered to be as a result of ignorance. They believe that only reasoned choices are moral and evil choices are not the best of choice. That is to say, a person who does evil or wrong does not understand a better way.

Though immorality is far from accepted in Stoicism, this philosophy accepts and acts in the interest of their neighbors and humanity at large no matter how immoral they are.

Choosing Virtue Ahead of Immorality

Having explained what Stoics believe virtue and immorality are, it is up to us as human beings to choose which is preferable and better for us and humanity in general.

Choosing virtue over immorality is certainly the ultimate path to achieving happiness or eudemonia according to the Stoics. Virtue in this sense is very necessary and sufficient for happiness, that is to say, virtue (wisdom, justice, self-control, and courage) is all you need to be happy and for you lead a happy life.

Choosing virtue ahead of immorality also gives us the idea that the concept of virtue (the only true good) creates a firm basis for strategic thinking and decision making in any given scenario. This has to do with patiently reflecting on the particular situation and properly using a form of virtue to respond to the situation. This goes to say, virtue helps us decide a proper way of reacting to different situations with truthfulness, gentleness, wisdom, and courage.

Virtue also creates a form of acceptance in our lives as human beings. With the idea of virtue in mind, one is likely to accept all the trial of life as they come our way. The situation where one can't accept the trials they face is what leads to sadness, depression, anger, and heartbreak, which are the order of today.

In essence, choosing virtue ahead of morality gives us the ability to control our desires and fears with wisdom, hence creating a lifestyle devoid of sadness and pain - in other words, happiness.

Choosing virtue ahead of immorality helps us focus on the generality of humanity and everyone we come in contact with. With the ideology of kinship and familiarity at heart, Stoics are just in their actions and, this in most cases provides a better way to act in a given situation. If Stoicism is embraced by humanity and virtuous act are chosen over immoral acts, compassion will be the order of the day as Stoicism encourages the idea of compassion.

Immorality, on the other hand, is generally associated with evil, badness, and wickedness. Now, in the law of the universe, you get what you give - or in other words, you reap what you sow. Therefore, in this situation, if you sow evil, wickedness, and badness, you will likely reap any of those.

This goes to show you that the choice of immorality only leads to pain, badness and sadness - not happiness. This is another reason to choose virtue ahead of immorality.

Going further, many modern-day analysts and scholars believe that Stoicism is the best choice of philosophy that should be practiced by humanity in a world where there are many terrible vices and in a world where lives are being lost daily. This philosophy is highly recommended because of its teachings of oneness and virtue.

Following the teachings of Marcus Aurelius, it is safe

to come to the conclusion that Stoicism is the best option for the state of our world today. These teachings emphasize treating all humans as family, with his belief that error in judgments is not an intentional act. He further teaches that a Stoic cannot be hurt by others; they can only hurt themselves through a vicious response.

Stoicism promotes the belief that everyone can develop virtue as virtues are not dependent on inborn qualities, background, or intellectual education. It is believed that every human being possesses an innate quality that lets us separate the good from the bad/evil. This quality can only be developed. Development in itself is a virtuous act. They further stress that the general idea of development and the major role of development is a life-long journey, not just a transition into adulthood.

To top it all, the similarity we all have as human beings is the ability to embark on a journey to gain progress. This journey can also be said to be a journey of virtue. It is important to also note that this ancient philosophy of Stoicism has positively impacted many modern ideologies and theories about ethics. It also provides an alternative system for guidance in life.

Flip through the next pages as we continue to help you on your quest to be happy.

Chapter Six

Eliminating Emotions

It is important to note that the popular notion that Stoics are emotionless cows standing under the rain is a totally false statement or notion. Having the ability to control one's emotion and be rationale in given situations is important and very necessary for every Stoic to know. But this doesn't define a Stoic or Stoicism as a philosophy. The key message of Stoicism is not to build an emotionless machine or to eliminate emotions but to know and learn to live life the best possible way.

In other words, the principle of emotions is like that of virtue in Stoicism; it is important and essential to achieving happiness but it is not the main message of Stoicism, rather living life the right way is the main aim of this ancient philosophy.

The principle of emotions is one of the major aspects of Stoicism. This principle simply revolves around the ability for Stoics to live through life without letting emotions like sadness, anger, pain, and distress affect their way of life or a decision that needs to be taken (rationality or indifference). It is the ability to accept the trials of life without letting them affect your daily routines. In other words, bad things will happen, but that shouldn't hold you back because life will always continue.

Emotions in Stoicism

Emotion in Stoicism goes deeper than the popular notion that Stoics repress or suppress emotion, when in fact, Stoics believe that a well-lived life is an outcome of joy and tranquility. As students and practitioners, Stoics learn and understand how we fit into the universe, which includes all the difficult and strange interactions of life.

Emotions are an affective state of mind where a being experiences hate, joy, sorrow, or fear. Emotions are distinguished from volitional and cognitive states of consciousness.

Despite the fact that a human mind is an impressive tool, Stoics understand that emotions are just part of the mental framework. Emotions are given regard in Stoicism, but are not given full regard, and decisions are based on rationality.

Stoics have a unique approach to the issue of emotions. Take, for instance, if there is hard rain pouring down on a Monday, you don't sit back at home and relax. You grab an umbrella or raincoat and find a way to work. This logic is exactly how emotions work in Stoicism. That is to say Stoics do not let emotions define and guide their behaviors; they just treat it like a rainy day, get an umbrella and move on.

In Stoicism, a person is expected to act well even when experiencing a strong, negative emotion like anger. Stoics believe that a feeling like anger or outburst is irrelevant, as it could have been avoided in the first place because anger itself is a result of taking up an unhealthy perspective which is against Stoic doctrines. Another reason why anger would be an irrelevant option for a Stoic is that they will actually opt for virtue over a bad feeling or emotion, hence avoiding anger.

Stoicism acknowledges three good feelings or emotions in their doctrine called "hai eupatheiai" in the Greek language. These three good feeling were created in contrast to the passion which can also be referred to as "bad feelings."

Below is the list of the three good feelings in contrast with the three bad feelings.

1. Joy versus Pleasure

2. Wish versus Lust/Appetite

3. Caution versus Fear.

The above list is definitely an odd one; but with a lot of background info and research, we should be able to deduce why the ancient Stoics came to these conclusions.

Joy versus Pleasure

Joy according to Stoics is attained by the wise, while pleasure, on the other hand, is considered to be a vice.

In Stoicism, Joy is seen as the elevation of spirit as a result of truth in goodness and truth in possession. For instance, Joy is when one first holds their child in their arms. This scene is considered a joyful one, not because of the immediate feeling you derive from it but the fact that the feeling of joy will never cease and never change to an opposite situation.

Pleasure, on the other hand, is not like the joy that lasts for a long time. It is usually a short satisfaction that can be taken away from you quickly.

In order words, joy is like true happiness that can last a long time, while pleasure is only for a period of time. That is to say, true peace isn't derived from external things, but rather from joy within.

Wish versus Lust/Appetite

To answer the question of why the Stoics consider wishing a good emotion and lust or appetite a bad one, we have to reference back to one of Marcus Aurelius' quotes which goes like this, "Consider the activity it is possible for you to carry out." This quote simply explains that Stoics consider pinning for things you don't have as a bad habit and a waste of time.

Stoics define appetite as a desire or pursuit of an expected situation in an irrational way. (Let's not forget that one of the bases of Stoicism is rationality). For example, enmity is an appetite for revenge and greed is an appetite for material things.

The feeling of appetite is unacceptable in Stoicism as the energy and fantasy derived from this feeling only promote unproductive actions. Don't forget that Stoics don't base their happiness on things that are out of their hands; so it is preferable to wish rather than have an appetite for something.

Why Do Stoics Prefer Wish Over Appetite?

Wish in Stoicism has to do with wanting something, but being contented whether you get it or not. In order words, your contentment is not based on possessing what you want, which is the case in appetite. Wish is a situation of appreciating and wanting the many good things of life -but not letting those many good things become your source of contentment.

Caution versus Fear

Caution versus fear takes the same logic as joy versus pleasure. Fear is an irrational way of avoiding expected danger. Fear suppresses the contentment we feel in the present because we think it will be taken away from us later. Now in Stoicism, this feeling of fear is classified as an irrelevant and unnecessary irrationality.

Caution, on the other hand, has to do with

preparation. Stoics believe that with caution, a person should understand that life is filled with ups and down and as a result of this, preparations should be laid down for all the difficulties of life. In order to properly progress in life, we have to approach the world with wariness and awareness.

Emotional Control

Having understood the idea of emotions in Stoicism, the feelings that are accepted and those that are considered wrong, we can safely conclude that a Stoic has the capacity to apply reason to their every action. This is to say, emotions will definitely arise, but these emotions will be subject to rationality and virtue - virtues being wisdom, courage, moderation, and justice.

So basically, in Stoicism, its practitioners are taught to regard desire, passion, and any form of emotion as indifferent.

Here's a quote from Marcus Aurelius' book, *Meditation*, to further explain the concept of emotional control in Stoicism:

"Make sure that the ruling and sovereign part of your soul remains unexpected by every movement, smooth or violent, in your flesh and that it does not combine with them, but circumscribes itself and restricts these experiences to the bodily parts.

Whenever they communicate themselves with the mind by virtue of that other sympathy as is bound to occur in a unified organism, you should not attempt to resist the temptation which is a natural one, but you must not allow the ruling center to add its own further judgment that the experience is good or bad." (Meditation 5.26)

This goes to say that Stoics have the ability to feel emotions to the highest degree, but with restrictions. Virtue should always be on stand by to put these emotions in check. In essence, this explanation is what is regarded as emotional control in this ancient philosophy.

Furthermore, Stoicism and actions are considered to work hand in hand. A Stoic is always prepared to act; he does not wait. He acts despite the difficulty and the challenge of the situation at hand. This is because, over time, a Stoic or Sage has been able to practice the power to overcome different emotional barriers.

Finally, what makes a wise man unique and different from a foolish man is his ability to put whatever happens to him to the test of his reasoning and act with a rational response. Emotions, if not controlled, might be the end of us. A lot of hasty decisions and judgments have left a lot of people in deep trouble. Thus, one should be able to separate their emotions from clouding their judgment.

Eliminating emotions is the beginning of reaching greater heights in one's life. Eliminating emotions is the pathway that leads to being logical, which is our next chapter. Immerse yourself in logical reasoning at all times, and watch yourself grow in grace and happiness.

Chapter Seven

Being Logical at All Times

Stoicism over the years has finally been recognized for its many contributions to the philosophy of the mind. One of the key principles of Stoicism that have been linked with the modern day philosophy of the mind is the ability of Stoics to be logical in their thinking at all times.

Logic

Logic in Stoicism is based on preposition logic. This deals with the use of facts and argument flow. The fact here simply has to do with truth and false of a situation. Stoically, preposition logic is referred to as assertables.

Background of Stoic Logic

The Stoics' philosophy of logic was regarded as one of the greatest and most generally accepted philosophies out of two in the classical world. By the 4th century BCE, the Stoic logic philosophy started to originate in a philosophical school called the Megarian school. Diodorus Cronus and his pupil, Philo, developed their own theories of Modality and cognitive prepositions.

Zeno, the father of Stoicism, also studied under the Megarian school and was said to be a fellow pupil like

Philo. He applied the philosophy of logic to Stoicism, but it was this philosophy, largely propounded and promoted by the third head of Stoic teachings in the third century BCE , Chryssipus of Soli. Chryssipus' Stoic logic was largely based on the analyzing of situations based on prepositions (true or false).

An integral and important part of the logic in Stoicism is assertability. That goes to say the basic unit of a Stoic logic is an assertable. Assertables are contents of a statement which have a truth value in the sense that, at any time, the statement is true or false. Stoic logic focuses on analyzing choices and consequences, hence creating preposition with connections like "if and then" "either and or" and "nit both." These connections are part of daily reasoning.

Logic is the aspect of Stoicism that examines and analyzes reason. Going further, we can say that for a person to achieve a happy and worthy life, they have to apply logical reasoning with their actions. Stoics also believe that to understand ethics, one has to apply logic to their thoughts and reasoning.

Brand Inwood described the stoics to believe that, "Logic helps a person see the case, reason effectively about practical ideas, stand his or her ground amid confusion, differentiate the certain from the probable, and so forth".

We all have those moments when we say or do

something foolish because our emotions made us. You decide to wait for the last minute to finish your work because you'd rather watch Breaking Bad, resulting in a last-minute panic. Or you lean in to kiss a friend because it felt right, only to be pushed away. If nothing else, emotions make life interesting.

But for the most part, we like to think that we're rational decision makers. To make choices, we consider our options and chose the one that makes the most sense. We're not willy-nilly about such things. And those foolish, emotion-based decisions are a rarity, not the norm. As Samuel Johnson once said, "We may take Fancy for our companion, but must follow reason as our guide."

Moreover, most of our public discourse assumes that we are rational. Philosophy, in particular, has tended to focus on logic and reason. The Stoics are one famous example, but Socrates also prided logic over emotion, even to the point of death. Some exceptions exist, like Nietzsche and Rousseau, but they are precisely that - exceptions.

Indeed, most of us like to think that we control our destiny with a rational choice—whether it's in buying a car or choosing a profession—but research shows we may not be as rational as we think.

To understand this fact first requires us to change our view on emotions. Most people see emotions in light of the feelings attached to them—the subjective experience of being happy, sad, or otherwise. When people are sad, they feel sad. It's a subjective mental state, nothing more.

Being logical doesn't mean we should let go of our emotions. As a matter of fact, we can't. No matter how we much feel we can stay away from the tons of emotions we feel every day, we will only end up deceiving ourselves in the long run. However, we can tweak our minds with respect to how we want it to feel.

When we apply logic in our daily life, we ensure things are done in an appropriate manner. Decisions are made only after weighing the consequences, actions are executed only after checking how they will influence the future. Now, that is the right way of doing things. If we end up rushing into something without properly taking a good look at it, we might be jumping into what is not right for us.

Logic is being applied to our daily lives. Talk about economic life, psychological well-being, in relationships, at work, at the shop - in fact, in anything we do. Stoics see logic as the will to reason. Practice Stoicism in your life and watch how you will start placing logic to every of your decision.

Logic is life itself. The great men you adore today applied logic more than a few times in the course of their lives. Thus, if you would wish to emulate them, be sure to hold logic very close to you.

Chapter Eight

Living a Stress-Free Life

In the previous chapters, we discussed how to remain completely happy by following the philosophy of the Stoics. Eliminating sentiments and emotions, staying true to logical reasoning, irrespective of the magnitude and attachment the situation or circumstance may hold, and sticking closely with virtue instead of immorality, is the key to real peace and happiness.

I'm sure you are familiar with the saying "one good turn deserves another," right? And also "what goes around surely comes back around?" Well, that is what Stoicism preaches. Be good to one another, but definitely not emotional to the point of being influenced by your feelings.

All these translate to one thing; living a stress-free life. Stress is both a necessary and unnecessary fatigue which builds up in our bodies due to many reasons we know or we don't even know. Stress can be accumulated in our body via a continuous stressful activity we keep engaging ourselves in. It can also be psychological.

As a matter of fact, stress can take on different forms, in the long run, achieving the same purpose -

making you feel down, tired, and unhappy. A lot of surveys and studies have been carried out over the years amongst adults on the levels of self-reported stress and the results came out quite overwhelming and alarming.

Many of them complained of stress from their work due to pressure mounted on them by their superiors or even employers. Some of them complained of the economy as their stress-motivating factor. Others laid their blame on their relationships, thereby feeling stressed in the long run.

Mind you, this book is not to give you a solution on how to bounce back economically. If that is your motive, then you are obviously in the wrong place. However, it will give you an insight on how to lift that pressure and stress off your chest, thereby making you feel free, glowing with joy, and most importantly, become truly happy.

Now, here is a question you should ask yourself. Are you stressed? If I am, what should I do? It is important to know that drinking a whole bottle of champagne won't wash your stress away, nor would swimming in the pool of cannabis wash off the stench of stress from your body. What you can do is quite simple – practice Stoicism.

It the best ticket you can get to take you out of that mess. And guess what? Stoicism is absolutely free. I'm sure you are more familiar with the term now than before, especially after reading through our previous educative and informative chapters. But let's do a quick recap, shall we?

Stoicism is a total way of life - the gateway to achieving complete happiness and tranquility. It encompasses esteemed areas of philosophy like ethics, physics, virtue, nature, and so many more. It focuses on the relationship between man and nature. It is also attributed to living a good and happy life. When you are a Stoic, you make logical decisions and judgments devoid of emotions and sentiments.

Be that as it may, living according to nature guarantees us a stress-free life. When you live life just as the creator had created us to have lived it, you are bound to be completely free from stress of any kind. And that entails being good to our fellow humans and nature in general. That is the only way we can live a stress-free life.

Rationality, zeal to succeed, seeking knowledge, understanding of the cosmos, and so much more are all part of Stoicism. If we behave the way we are truly meant to behave, then we will be extremely and supremely happy. This will, in turn, make living very easy and stress-free.

How to Live a Stress-Free Life Stoically

1.   Control Your Situation: Have you ever wondered why lots of people end up not getting anything right in their lives? Why do they keep failing at everything they have tried working on? Why do they just feel stressed after many trials and end up giving up so easily? It's because they don't have control of the situation. No one has total control of his or her situation more than one who beats an addiction.

Firstly, know the things you have control over. It is important to make this distinction, then differentiate it from what we don't have control over. For instance, if watching porn is what you can not control, irrespective of how hard you try to gain control over it, then it's better we differentiate that from the others.

Knowing these differences between your strength and weaknesses is an added advantage.

2.   Know the Real Problem from Abstract Ones: Imaginary problems and issues have given lots of people more stress than the present ones. I'm sure we are very popular with these words "what if..." We now start getting worried over what is not even a problem to begin with. Then stress starts accumulating in our bodies.

"What is" should really be the concern of our life and not "what might." If we actually start thinking of the present problems in our lives, we will realize that our minds would be focused on finding a solution. But an imaginary problem causes us undeserved and unnecessary stress.

We might be broke tomorrow, but we still have something to hold on to today. We might be homeless tomorrow, but we still have a good house that gives us shelter today. We might be jobless tomorrow, but let's focus on today's job which puts food on our table. Thus, do not start feeling pressured unnecessarily.

3. Know What You Need: Knowing the things you need is vital in living a stress-free life. What are the things you really need? Have you ever taken a moment to think deeply about that question? Don't think in a materialist manner, but as a rational human being.

What are the things you really need to live a happy life? Does keeping a large circle bring you happiness? How about living a materialistic life? Would it make your life less stressful? These and more are the important questions we need to ask ourselves in order to know what we really want.

It is important to know that gaining a stress-free life Stoically is not an easy journey. It means we live our lives while letting go of desires, pleasures, and pains. Forgoing these desires and wants might seem confusing at first, but in the long run, it is for our own good.

4. Cultivate Your Inner Self: All that we are trying to discuss boils down to your inner self. Having total control of your condition and situation is the key to living a stress-free life. You will agree with me that we are not in control of the economy. We are also not in control of what happens in the next five minutes of our lives.

Additionally, we are not in control of our relationships. But one thing we can control is our state of mind and how we make our decisions and judgments. How we relate with other people and nature in general, and our drive towards living a good life will determine if we will end up being happy or not.

A true Stoic believes that a peasant can be most happy if he lives the life of a Sage. On the other hand, a king could live a miserable life unless he ends up living like a Sage. The rules of living are quite different from that of a peasant to a king.

Where a king has many opportunities to lead a good life, a peasant is only limited to few opportunities. In other words, our opportunities for living a good life vary, yet it is only possible for one who has total control of his or her inner self.

A stress-free life is all we all want, no matter the method we decide to follow. Whether we pay a therapist to talk us through it or we practice Stoicism all by ourselves, the end result will still be the same – wanting a stress-free life. With that being said, do not allow depression to take that sanity away from you.

Yes, you saw that right; DEPRESSION! Read on to the next chapter as we open your mind on how to overcome this silent evil.

Chapter Nine

Beating Depression with Stoicism

According to the words of Marcus Aurelius, "Never let the future disturb you. You will meet it, if you have to, with the same weapons of reason which today arm you against the present."

This statement says it all. Why feel depressed when the future is still far? Most times, we forget that we have no control over some things in our lives. Thus, we end up hurting ourselves, feeling really depressed, and shutting everyone out of our lives.

Depression, according to a concise English dictionary is the mental state characterized by a pessimistic sense of inadequacy and despondent lack of activity. In other words, it is a sunken stage in a person's life which is characterized by sad feelings of gloom and inadequacies. If you happen to find yourself or a friend curling up alone in the confines of a bed, looking dejected and hopeless, then you or that particular person is depressed.

Depression eats deep and is present in a person for a long time before it manifests. The pain one feels is directed inward, with lots of negative thoughts running through the mind. Life will feel meaningless, if not a waste of space.

One would start withdrawing into their shells and comfort zones. Your life would seem like an embarrassment, even to you. And there would be no better way of ending it all than to take one's life. In as much as depression is real and present in today's world, it is not true to say that depression cannot be curbed and managed.

It is a passing phase in one's life which could be passed successfully with the right means or methods. Talking and reaching out to friends helps, getting a new passion or hobby helps, and meeting new people is also great. But one method that works fast and adequately is following the philosophy and tenets of Stoicism.

We often complain about how life has been unfair, but forget to check ourselves on how to live life in the best possible manner. Stoicism presents us with the perfect alternative for a better life. Now the question remains, are we making good use of this alternative? Are we even trying to live a good life?

Depression comes after we had made a grave mistake in the course of our lives; after we have failed to make great decisions and judgments concerning our lives. That is when depression will begin to set in. It's not the relationship we hold dear that hates us. It is how we relate to these several phenomena that depict our lives.

Stoicism teaches us to be logical in all areas of our

lives. It puts logic ahead of sentiments and emotions. It also places virtue high before immorality. Following this way of life will definitely keep depression far away from you. This is why we often imagine why our lives seem to be regressing instead of making progress.

We often picture ourselves at a very high point many years from now and end up moving a little, or not moving at all, toward that point. This is characterized by our way of making decisions and judgments. Change that today and watch yourself grow.

Always be filled with positivity. Negative thoughts or pessimism have a way of pulling us back no matter the amount of hard work we put in. Positivity brings the whole world to our feet. It makes us see anything as achievable no matter the obstacles around it.

Therefore, curbing depression with Stoicism comes with two important questions that must be answered in order to achieve good results. First, we need to ask ourselves where those silly emotions we often feel each time depression wants to set in come from. According to a study conducted by a popular Austrian Neurologist, Sigmund Freud, divided psyche into three parts and he named these parts; ID, EGO, and SUPEREGO.

The ID is the part that holds the instinctive, aggressive, and jealous kinds of emotions. The ID also creates anxiety, especially if the ID is threatened. For instance, ID emotions occur when an over-pampered child gets angry, or even sad. The emotions rage powerfully and quite short.

SUPER-EGO emotions are criticizing oneself. It comes as a result of comparing yourself with another. It also comes with self-loathing, self-criticism, and trying to make yourself into a perfectionist, while EGO is the emotion that erupts while trying to create a balance between both emotions. This is the enemy of man. It is the combination of emotions that might end up overpowering you in the long run.

Stoicism is the realistic solution toward these surges of emotion. It is the only clean, clear method you can use in curbing depression and living a happy life. It builds up your mind to be indifferent to pain and pleasure. It gives you peace of mind, something prayers, hopes, and the words "don't worry," would never give you. Go through the writings of Marcus Aurelius, Epictetus, Seneca, and many other Stoic philosophers.

Immerse yourself to their teachings and life lessons. Your life will definitely take shape - a very nice shape. Stoicism would give you a pathway toward accepting nature. It prepares your mind for the worst. Life can be quite tough. Thus, Stoicism will prepare your mind to stay clear-headed and maintain complete focus in reaching your set out goals.

In the words of Nassim Nicholas Taleb, "A Stoic is

someone who transforms fear into prudence, pain into transformation, mistakes into initiation, and desires into undertaking."

That way, one would maintain indifference to the pains and hardships of life, thereby remaining focus and clear-headed. In other words, our path would be set right before us, and our mistakes would be perceived and corrected. Stoicism helps us point out which part of our decisions are clearly irrational. It serves as a guiding principle toward making better judgments. It preaches to us about taking a second look at our decisions and judgments before executing them.

How to overcome depression

1. **Inner Control:** According to the words of Epictetus, we should "Remember, it is not enough to be hit or insulted to be harmed, you must believe that you are being harmed. If someone succeeds in provoking you, realize your mind is complicit in the provocation. Which is why it is essential that we do not respond impulsively to impressions; take a moment before reacting, and you will find it easier to maintain control."

No Stoic principle beats having inner control of oneself. It is important to know that one's thoughts are exactly what one needs to master before gaining control of the total body. For example, you can train your mind to start thinking positively and seeing life from a whole new angle. Thus, the kind of thoughts your mind would produce would be definitely toward the way you had configured it.

Controlling oneself can be quite difficult, especially when one has an addiction. However, even after configuring our thinking style, we might still find it very difficult to resist being influenced by our emotions. Therefore, practicing Stoicism continuously is the key to having total control of the mind, which will in turn help in creating a stress free life for us all.

2. **Personal Responsibility:** As Marcus Aurelius rightly puts it, "And see that you keep a cheerful demeanor and retain your independence of outside help and the peace which others can give. Your duty is to stand straight – not held straight."

Many times, we have done things that we aren't even proud of, thus, looking the other way. Many times we have neglected our sense of responsibility not because we don't want to but because we are ashamed to. This is against Stoicism. We all are accountable to our deeds and actions.

We need to take charge of our lives if really we want to live a happy and stress-free life. Challenge yourself to making the right decisions, so as not to be burdened with taking responsibility for what you aren't proud of. You are your own master. Instead of being the normal complainer, Stoicism will teach you to be an actual rational thinker as you face your problems.

The feeling that comes with taking responsibility is quite amazing.

3.   The Future/Success: Dreaming about a beautiful and amazing future just won't do the trick for you. Don't get me wrong, dreaming is quite good. As a matter of fact, it is the first thing great men do before achieving their insurmountable feats. So dream of the future with big success, but are you ready to make that dream a reality?

No matter the outcome of your dream, whether good or bad, sitting down and doing nothing or even giving up after the first try is not the right way to go about it. Remember, Stoics do not give up. Keep striving hard, keep pushing, keep working, until you see the light. What Stoicism will do is configure your mind positively, so as to be strong and not be influenced with your emotions, because trust me, fear would come.

To this effect, allow me to end this with the golden words of Marcus Aurelius. "Have the acts of a man with an eye for precisely what needs to be done, not in the glory of its doing."

4.   Death: Seneca once said, "Death: there's nothing bad about it at all except the thing that comes before it – the fear of it."

Death shouldn't be a thing of fear for us, but instead something that should boost our morale and hope in living a better life. Many of us get scared the moment death is being mentioned. Little wonder why people gather more in a celebration than in a funeral. But, like it or not, death is inevitable.

But the real question you should ask yourself is, what then should we do with our life before death comes knocking on our door? Are we going to keep being depressed or dust of our behind and start taking charge of our lives? Stoicism will help you focus on life itself; how best to utilize every breath you take in and out. How you can make your life meaningful to you and nature

Depression is real in case many of you don't believe so. Have you ever been in a state where everything starts going from bad to worse? Nothing hurts more than that feeling. You start feeling like a loser, like your life is a total joke. Be that as it may, Stoicism will help you beat it and give you the real happiness you truly deserve.

Chapter Ten

Being Calm Amidst Adversities

What many of us lack is the ability to remain calm and collected even in the face of adversities, tribulations, and obstacles. Great men don't fidget, no matter the circumstances. They remain focused and geared toward doing something great or achieving a massive feat for themselves. That is one secret they will never tell you.

Only a few would like to share the secret to their success and happy life. Zeno of Citium faced lots of criticism in the course of propagating his philosophy. Apple's big man, Steve Jobs also faced his own tribulations before becoming the co-founder of one of the world 's leading gadget-producing company.

This same process goes for all other great men before climbing to the position of authority and power. As a child, Aliko Dangote, the most successful black man alive, sold sweets in school as a young boy. He remained calm and in control of his life before things turned to his favor years later.

Being a stoic comes with its own share of problems. Life is not going to be nice because you made a resolution to be good and live by virtue. But, don't let it weigh you down; instead remain calm. This is one of the qualities of a true Stoic; the ability to remain calm and still maintain the relationship between yourself and nature, even when things go south.

Life often comes up with events that may seem to be over us. The more we solve these problems, the more other ones keep springing up. Stoicism will help you establish stability and control over your life. Why create problems for ourselves when we can actually avoid them completely if we practice Stoicism?

To be fair, most of these problems we find ourselves with are creations of our own doing. If only we could keep records of our daily lives and activities, we would be able to pinpoint the errors and mistakes we make every single day. Thus, Stoicism keeps your focus instead of derailing from your goal. It charges you up until you feel calm, in control, and secure.

Even in the face of tribulations, learn to separate your emotions, feelings, passion, and desires. This will give you a clear head to sail through the raging tides of adversities right before you. Stoicism principles teach us that life still continues even in the face of adversities. These principles should govern your mind as a Stoic, so that if failure looms, adaptation becomes necessary.

The ultimate goal of Stoicism is to give inner peace to man. Achieving this inner peace comes from dealing with problems calmly and maturely. However, in order to scale through a problem, we must understand that problem first. We must be able to transform our problems into the fuel that feeds our fires.

Epictetus rose from a slave to a philosopher. However, this didn't come easy. He had to master his present condition before transforming it into his blessing. The same goes for Marcus Aurelius. He faced lots of tribulations like any Stoic you will find. Yet, he stayed calm amidst those adversities. Seneca was also a statesman who had written lots of letters and essays on the importance of staying calm amidst adversities.

Do you want to live life like this great Stoic thinkers? Then immerse yourself to these three philosophies:

1. Accept That Emotions Come From Within: Marcus Aurelius wrote, "Today I escaped anxiety. Or no, I discarded it, because it was within me, in my own perceptions – not outside."

It is important to know that outside forces can not influence or make us feel bad. The emotions we feel come from within (inside us). It is very easy to lay blame on the outside world and phenomena, but the truth remains, all conflicts begin from within.

When we run away from our problems, from reality, we tend to prolong these problems in our lives, thereby harming ourselves even more. Thus, the next time you find yourself deep in a problem, don't look at the outside for solution, but look inward. Thus, instead of running away from your problems, face them instead.

2. Get a Mentor That Teaches You Honesty: One of the greatest virtues is honesty. Honesty in words and deeds can take you out of nowhere to somewhere. According to the words of Seneca, "Choose someone whose way of life as well as words, and whose very face as mirroring the character that lies behind it, have won your approval. Be always pointing him out to yourself either as your guardian or as your model. This is a need, in my view, for someone as a standard against which our character can measure themselves. Without a ruler to do it against you won't make it crooked straight."

Check yourself first before choosing who to be your mentor. You and your mentor must have something in common – same goals, same beliefs, or same ideology. That way, you can be sure to blend in with the ways of your guardian. For example, as a writer, you might want to get someone that would guide you on your path to being formidable in the field of writing.

You might want someone to brush your crude skills and pull you through until you come out better. Irrespective of your profession, situation, and circumstance, there is always someone you can learn a thing or two from. Immerse yourself within their life; learn lessons from their stories and works, their successes and failures, their strengths and weaknesses, and so much more.

One important thing to know is that this is not a competition nor a comparison. As a matter of fact, it isn't about using the life of your mentor as a benchmark or yardstick for reaching your goals. Also, even after emulating our mentor, our lives might not be exactly what we want or success might not come immediately. Therefore, stay calm and be patient. Everyone has someone they can look up to.

3. Acknowledge Life after Failure: The failure of a man is not the end of his life. Even after failing, one must pick himself back up and forge ahead continuously. Abraham Lincoln, who became the president of the United States in 1960, also had his fair share of failures which he didn't let deter him from reaching his goal.

He lost more than he won and still, he is celebrated to date. According to the words of Marcus Aurelius, "Does what happened to keep you from acting with justice, generosity, self-control, sanity, prudence, honesty, humility, straightforwardness, and all other qualities that allow a person's nature to fulfill itself? So remember this principle when something threatens to cause you pain: the thing itself is no misfortune at all; to endure it and prevail is great good fortune."

People won't always give you a pat on the back for every idea that comes out of your head. Most times, they will even criticize you and tag you a failure. That shouldn't get to you. Instead, transform this failure into something great in order to come out even better and stronger.

How to Remain Calm with Stoicism

1. **Live in the Present:** Have you ever thought about the future? What life holds for you in the next five to ten years of your life? These and many more questions are what puts fear and anxiety into us, thereby making us lose focus on the present. We forget that our present makes the future.

   Most times, we are mostly carried away by the glitters and glamour of life. We tend to get carried away by what life offers. For example, the rise of technology has brought the likes of sophisticated gadgets and devices which can be very distracting. Let's cultivate the habit of being in the present and make the best out of what we have and where we find ourselves.

2. **Be Thankful:** Always be thankful to people around you, no matter the circumstances. It is the little gratitude you give that will lead to higher altitudes. Most times, we tend to not give actual thanks to the people behind our smiles and successes, especially if things start going our way. We will now start thinking it's our effort and hard work that got us where we are.

That might be true. But one thing that is also true is that you alone didn't achieve the feat. Be thankful even to the smallest person that helped you climb the ladder to success. Saying thank you doesn't even cost a thing. But the effect it holds on people is quite scintillating.

Be thankful for everything you've got. Be thankful for who ever stood by you through trying times or difficult moments. Be thankful for the food you eat. Be thankful for your family standing by you. There are more than a thousand things we should be thankful for every day of our lives. Cultivate the habit of being thankful and watch yourself grow.

3. **Eliminate Attachments:** Attachments, emotions, feelings, sentiments, and so on are all the same thing, no matter how much you try to twist the name. In the lives of the majority, these terms rule their world completely. Little wonder why they don't get to make good decisions and judgements, thereby causing them to make mistakes that may cause them something grave in the long run.

Stoicism preaches their elimination from our lives. A total elimination of these terms in our lives will find us calm, even in the face of adversities. We will be able to face any tribulations or obstacles standing in our way, without fidgeting.

4. **Hold Time Dear:** Time is everything, but time waits for no one. Technology and science have been able to invent sophisticated and scintillating machines, ideas, and so much more. But one of the things they haven't been able to invent is the machine to stop time. Thus, my friend, hold time dear.

However, we are not saying you start hurrying through life. We are also not saying you start jumping some steps, cutting corners, and even duplicating phases just to reach your goal faster and illegitimately. That wouldn't be right and cool.

Instead, always ensure you are doing the right thing at the right time. Efficiency and effectiveness should be your right hand men. Always have it at the back of your mind that death can come for us at any time. Thus, use it as a guiding factor toward reaching your goals.

5. **Stop Procrastinating; Do it Now:** Procrastination has a way of making us lazy and useless in the long run. Imagine shifting an hour work for as long as ever knowing fully well that it is vital to our survival. Crazy right? When we start saying "I'll do it later," we are creating room for a beast

of laziness in us.

We won't realize that until we start seeing the damage delay had done to us. Ensure you cultivate the habit of doing it now. That is when your life will take shape. If we start doing everything at the exact time we ought to have done it, our life will definitely become far better than the way it is. Procrastination will definitely hold you back from achieving this.

6. **Prioritize:** Even in Economics, there is room for making your topmost priority list. This is called a Scale of Preference. Take your time and make your scale of preference. Start from the least important things in your life and end with the most important things you hold dear.

Notwithstanding, we don't have to get rid of anything before we make our priorities right. The reason why we've not been making that progress we had envisioned is because of our misplaced priorities. Instead of letting go of what drags us behind, let's try and look for a whole new angle.

What exactly can we do to make those things become useful to us? For example, social media can be quite crazy. The glamour, the limelight, the attention, and so much more, can be quite intriguing and deceiving. Even if it may slow your progress, you can't say you'd want to throw it away all of a sudden. Instead, tweak your activities on it to make your life more colorful.

7. **Be Honest:** Honesty in words and deeds is a trait that can be very hard to come by in this modern world we live in. People hardly tell the truth these days. They believe being honest will do nothing but get you killed. That might be true. But isn't it better to die honorably than to live as a pathetic liar?

Try and see through yourself and check that you are clean before you start laying criticism on others around you. Be a good example to others by following the path of honesty and righteousness. That is the only way you will be calm even in the face of adversities. When your hands are clean, you'll have nothing to worry about.

Follow these guidelines and watch how calmness will reign over you completely, even in the face of adversity. Train your mind, don't cut corners, and accept everything as the will of God. That is the only way you can truly be happy. The next chapter will include the true meaning of indifference. Read through as we clear all misconceptions and misrepresentations of the word "INDIFFERENCE."

Chapter Eleven

Indifference: Unveiling the Goodness in You

The word Stoicism has been considered synonymous with indifference more often not. Each time we hear the word Stoicism, indifference comes to mind. But the question we should ask ourselves is, "Indifference to what?" Most times, emotions are very hard to let go of. They come as a result of the way we absorb events and happenings around us.

A typical businessman would feel very bad at the sight of a loss, thereby losing focus on the business. This would be evident in the kinds of decisions he made henceforth. Indifference in Stoicism is a very large concept and equally provocative. A lot of people characterized it, with Stoics, to mean indifference to anything and everything.

Indifference to pleasure, indifference to pain, indifference to wealth, indifference to our emotions, and so much more. They now begin to think Stoics don't really care about anything at all. This is very wrong. It's the misconception and the misrepresentation of the concept propagated mostly by the modern Stoics.

Be that as it may, true Stoics aren't indifferent in

that manner at all. What indifference means to Stoics is that they believe and trust in the order of nature. This belief should be more than enough for one to stop feeling drawn toward expectations and desires.

A strong belief in fate strengthens one's indifferent stand. When you are indifferent, you don't need anything to go a certain and actual way. You just lay back, take a deep breath, and watch nature work its magic.

This is one perfect way of being stress-free, staying away from depression, and being genuinely happy. Stoicism gives you that push you need toward loving yourself. Indifference gives you the strength to push further without wanting the irrelevant freebies and bonuses. It builds your mind up to scaling through even greater obstacles in your life.

Indifference to the pain and pleasure of life comes as a result of configuring one's mind toward the path of eudemonia. Accept both good and evil as they come, knowing full-well that we can only do little or nothing to change it. As Marcus Aurelius rightly puts it, "Whatever happens to you has been waiting to happen since the beginning of time. The twining strands of fate wove both of them together: your own existence and the things that happen to you."

As an important concept of Stoicism, indifference comes with being calm and resilient toward our problems, the ability to pass through that phase without feeling any kind of emotion. Daniel, who is a janitor at a prestigious telecommunication firm, comes in smiling and goes out with no worries at all.

Many will always wonder what his secret was. Daniel doesn't even make up to six figures a year. He is also clearly not living the American dream, but he exudes so much love and happiness. Well, it's pretty simple! Daniel has found a new path to living a happy life. He has embraced Stoicism, thereby becoming indifferent to the events, happenings, and circumstances revolving around him.

Be that as it may, only a true and patient Stoic can attain complete indifference. This is the only way to achieve complete peace and serenity. According to Stoicism, it is not what you endure that matters, but how you endure it. Indifference is not only about accepting what life throws at us. It is about how well we handle and take care of the problems.

Thus, giving up is not an option with Stoics. Being depressed is also not an option. Let take an example from the life and lessons of Seneca, one of Stoicism's powerhouses. His friend, Lucilius, had sought his advice on more than one occasion. This particular experience was remarkable.

Lucilius, as a civil servant, had a lawsuit against him which would soil his reputation down the mud, thereby putting an end to his political career. Seneca writes him a letter, telling Lucilius to place himself in the worst possible situation, thereby preparing his mind for the worst possible outcome.

This helped Lucilius in seeing the situation from a whole new perspective, thereby becoming indifferent and accepting any possible outcome in clean faith. Indifference should be the cornerstone of all Stoic beliefs. Lucilius realized that Seneca was providing him with a path toward inner peace, reconciliation, and being comfortable even the midst of tribulations.

Others would have gone into depression - or even contemplated suicide in general. But instead, Seneca told his friend to consider the act of Stoicism. Seneca made an example of himself. He had also witnessed a great slump – an exile, ridicule, humiliation, and bankruptcy. Yet, he remained string, configured his mind into being indifferent, and came back even stronger.

The tribulations and struggles of our lives shouldn't be the end of everything for us. Instead, it should be the fuel that feeds our fire of survival. It should be the gateway toward the start of a new beginning. A stoic should always hope for the best while expecting the worst in any situation.

Be that as it may, go out there; embrace your life and all events that unfold afterward with open arms.

Feeling bad about anything won't change the outcome of the situation. Instead, make the best of it. Just like the saying goes, "When life throws you a lemon, you make lemonade."

Listen, we do not have control over everything that has happened or is even what is happening to us right now. Sometimes, we might not even know how these things happen. So, do not worry or even get sad about it. Instead, be sure to make the best out of the situation. Remember, there is nothing like giving up in the Stoics' dictionary. No matter how much you keep falling, learn to pick yourself back up every time.

Our level of tenacity and perseverance differs from each other. Thus, the rate at which we generally recoup from a loss, downfall, or even a disaster also differs. To this effect, what might work for you might not work for me. Try different Stoicism techniques as much as you want until you master your preferred techniques.

You might decide to meditate, retrace your steps back, and think about the previous decisions and judgements you've made. Walk through the park to clear your head, if possible. Do you have a car? Even better. Drive around and around until your start feeling yourself again. This would only mean one thing, trying to feel unperturbed.

The state of being unperturbed can also be known as ataraxia. It is the complete phase in our lives where we gain total freedom from worry, distress, and anger. In other words, it is known as having a peace of mind and being totally subdued by calmness and serenity. Reaching the state of atatraxia is the ultimate goal of every Stoic.

Nevertheless, pleasure is not something to flee from, at least not for Stoics. It is an important part of our life we must learn to understand and control. Only when we hold total control of it do we would know how and when to apply it in our daily lives. Additionally, pleasure can only be applied successfully and correctly if it is applied in line with virtue.

Virtue is the light that shines on the path of Stoicism. Pleasure without its guiding principle, virtue, would leave you reckless and irrational, thus making your life irresponsible. No one prays not to have or experience the pleasures of life. Life can be quite boring without pleasure, except if you are a monk.

Stoicism will show you the world in a whole new angle; that is being indifferent. You will definitely experience pain and pleasure, but how you react and control these emotions is what matters. Cultivate a strong mind and train yourself well in controlling your emotions toward pleasure or pain.

Failure to train yourself can lead to your downfall, or even ruin. However, a perfectly trained mind would be able to differentiate both pains and pleasures from influencing our emotions, thereby maintaining an indifferent stand when these emotions sprout out.

Just as what you hold dear today can be used against you, anything you once cherished can also be used against you if you don't play your cards right. Therefore, the only way to be on a safer side is not to even feel attached to anything in general. That way, it would be hard to have a weakness.

Thus, according to Seneca, enjoying the pleasures that come from our hard work or even good fortune is not a bad thing. However, we should always put it at the back of our mind that those things might turn against us someday. Also, we should develop a mind which would enable us to part with it anytime that happens.

With that being said, the key to living a Stoic life is indifference. Indifference unlocks the goodness in you. It opens up your eyes to what you are actually missing after making irrational decisions and judgments. Sometimes, we wish we paid a little more attention to being indifferent to the pains and pleasures of our lives. Indifference puts a stop to depression even before it manifests.

This brings us to our next chapter; practicalizing Stoicism in our daily lives. Trust me, the chapter is awesome and soul-captivating.

Chapter Twelve

A Pinch of Stoicism in Our Daily Lives

A pinch of Stoicism in our lives won't be a bad idea as we strive through the struggles of life. A pinch of goodness and indifference will surely help us maintain a happy and healthy lifestyle.

Like we pointed out in the previous chapters, knowing about Stoicism is not enough. How about studying it? What is the essence of knowing about something without practicing it in our daily lives? Thus, knowing and applying it are two different things entirely. It is the only way we can gain from Stoicism.

In today's world, many of us live our lives recklessly, with no purpose, passion, or drive. Some of us even end up getting depressed after making unwise decision. We keep trying the same methods and techniques that have failed us consistently. Aren't you tired of repeating the same thing over and over again?

Aren't you tired of getting the same heartbreaking results from the irrational decisions and judgments you make? Just a pinch of Stoicism would make a difference. Just a pinch of Stoicism will change your life miraculously. It will equip you with rationality and virtuousness. Here are some of the daily Stoic practices you can actually apply as you go about your daily life.

1. **Always Avoid Stress:** Marcus Aurelius writes, in *Meditations*, "You have power over your mind — not outside events. Realize this, and you will find strength."

Avoid anything that seems stressful or might cause you stress. Marcus Aurelius is telling us to always look inward for a solution to our problems. We all have the power to control our minds and thoughts one way or the other. Configure your mind in an amazing manner and seek the power to scale through any problem from within yourself. Do not forget to meditate if you have to.

How to Apply: While meditating, jot down your inner thoughts. This will help you remember everything after you are done meditating. Make sure you write out what you can control and what you cannot. The moment you do this, you'll have power over how you react that which you do not control. Trust me there is power in telling the difference between these two.

2. **Always Learn to Control Your Anger:** As Seneca puts it, "If a man is angry, let us give him time to come to realize what he has done: he will be his own critic."

One of the crazy feelings that had caused more harm than good is our anger. Sometimes, we end up doing dumb stuff just because our anger has taken over us completely. We now start seeing things differently and behaving violently. Seneca was of the opinion that an angry man will definitely see things clearly after he had calmed down.

How to apply: Meditation is the key to anger. Instead of lashing out, breaking things we bought with our money, and doing crazy things to anyone around us, how about you try solitude? When you are angry, always learn to talk less and keep to yourself more. Meditation will make us reach our inner self and give us the calmness we deserve. You can also take a walk or drive around to clear your head. It works.

3. Dealing with Difficult People: No matter how hard we try to avoid people, especially the ones that make our lives difficult, we just can't. They might be our bosses, our colleagues, our relatives, or even our friends. One would get to realize that we are stuck with these people and getting rid of them is not an option. But instead, we learn to get along with them.

Marcus Aurelius said, "Begin each day by telling yourself: Today I shall be meeting with interference, ingratitude, insolence, disloyalty, ill-will, and selfishness — all of them due to the offenders' ignorance of what is good or evil."

How to Apply: One thing we should take note of is that we cannot constantly influence people's decisions and opinions no matter how hard we try. Even if we are able to do that a few times, we won't be able to do that continuously. How about learning to cope with it? Be true and honest to yourself. Never compromise your values and everything will be fine.

When they see that, irrespective of how hard they try, you still remain yourself – humble, loyal, and honest, they will also learn to cope with you. However, continue to be yourself and on your best behavior. That is the only way to deal with difficult people.

4. Our Tribulations Can be Utilized: Ryan Holiday also said that, "The obstacle in the path becomes the path. Never forget, within every obstacle is an opportunity to improve our condition."

Our problems should be the stepping stones towards greatness. If great men of today backed out at the slightest challenge, the world wouldn't be what it is today. Believe it or not, challenges will come. They will come, especially when we least expect them. But, be sure to be ready at all times.

How to Apply: Imagine you are on the verge of getting a multi-million dollar contract with a telecommunication company, but faced a little challenge of facing bankruptcy at that same time. This scenario is a very tense and a crazy moment that will take the Stoic in us to pull through it. Now, would you allow the multi-million dollar contract that will enable you to keep your company from drowning disappear from your grasp or would do all it takes to win?

Stir obstacles in the right direction and they will end

up working for you. Make use of your experience and knowledge on how you tackle everyday problems.

5. Fail Sometimes: Marcus said that, "Does what's happened to keep you from acting with justice, generosity, self-control, sanity, prudence, honesty, humility, straightforwardness, and all other qualities that allow a person's nature to fulfill itself?"

There is no harm in falling down sometimes. We definitely can't win all the time. Thus, when something wants to start causing us pain because we'd fail, always remember this side of Stoicism.

What matters is that we stand up and get walking again. We recalculate our moves and steps, then come back stronger. It is important to know that there is always at least an atom of lesson in our failures. Don't feel pressured. Sometimes, the smell of too much victory and success can be quite intoxicating, thereby getting to our head. Fail sometimes; it will remind you of how hard is it to succeed.

How to Apply: Failure can be overwhelming most times, especially if you are not used to failing. You will now start feeling surprised and angry over your failure. Don't be carried away. Always learn to focus on the bigger picture. Don't feel saddened with everyone looking at you like a loser.

Gather strength from their criticism, learn deep

lessons, and know your mistakes. It's the result that matters, trust me. No one cares how many times you've failed. Be the winner everyone wants to associate with. Abraham Lincoln failed more than he won. Today, no one is celebrating him for those failures, but for his tenacity and perseverance to succeed.

Well, that and more are what it entails to live like a Stoic. Like we pointed out before, to know is to forget, to practice is to remember, and practice they say makes perfect. If we keep practicing, we are sure to reach the stage of eudemonia – real happiness according to Stoics. This brings us to our next chapter, how Stoicism opens up a pathway for real happiness, joy, and positivity.

Chapter Thirteen

Stoicism: A Pathway to Joy, Happiness, and Positivity

Happiness is the final outcome of Stoicism. It is why Zeno of Citium coined the philosophy in the first place. How can man truly be happy? What can man do to live a happy life? How does man influence nature into becoming truly happy? No matter how much you try to twist these questions, they will still bring us to one conclusion – Happiness.

We should know that obtaining happiness is not restricted to just one means. There are lots of means one can follow to attain real happiness, even if it may look weird in the beginning. For example, Negative Visualization is one effective way of experiencing happiness. As a matter of fact, early Stoics like Seneca, Epictetus, and Marcus Aurelius had used negative visualization to give themselves hope and happiness even in the face of severe obstacles.

What does Negative Visualization do? How does one visualize negatively in order to achieve long-deserved happiness? It's pretty simple. All we need to do it to configure our mind into picturing the bad side to everything revolving around us. What if things go south? What if it just doesn't go the way we had planned it?

This will certainly make you feel better in the long run and prepared for the worst. It will make you realize how lucky you have been with all the good things surrounding you, thereby encouraging you to count your blessings.

There is no better way of being grateful for the things you have than thinking along negative visualization. These thoughts will, therefore, trigger a grateful emotion in you which will, in turn, put a smile on your face. For example, when we think about all the homeless children which are a result of war, hunger, and destruction going on in their places, we tend to look up and thank God even for the little we have.

To that effect, we are bound to start thanking God for the good life we are enjoying, the peace we have in our environment, and the plenty and plush that surround us. This will, in turn, make us genuinely happy.

It is important to know that no matter how crazy or damaged you might appear to be, negative visualization will definitely give you a sense of gratitude. There is always someone out there who is poorer than you. There is always someone out there who is uglier than you. There is always someone out there who lacks the thing you have and whom you are far better than. So long as you are not dead, there is always a reason to be thankful and grateful.

Like we discussed earlier, negative visualization is the cover that makes you see the world from a whole new angle entirely. Even when we exaggerate our position in life in order to make us feel better, it actually supports it and helps us get exactly what we want – genuine happiness and peace of mind.

Additionally, Stoics are of the view that we can never find the real happiness that we deserve if we don't let go of expectations and hope. If we keep holding on to these two, there will surely be a problem. There is no way we will get a better and clearer picture of our future if we don't detach ourselves from these things.

Happiness should be seen as a present thing. It is not a future prospect. If we are focused on the future while neglecting today, there is no way we will be happy today. This can make us feel depressed and gloomy. At this point, nothing will make sense at all.

The Stoic remedy for this is reflected by the Ralph Ellison quote, "Life is to be lived, not controlled…"

If we keep that in mind, irrespective of how hard reality tries to control or influence our judgments and deductions, we will still remain indifferent and not attached, and we are sure to live a happy life. Additionally, if we stick to the plan of just controlling what is within our power and neglecting but knowing that which we cannot control, then that is the only way we can turn a blind eye to different tons of effect life will throw at us. There is dignity in accepting things as they come.

According to Seneca, "No insane person can be happy, and no one can be sane if he regards what is injurious as the highest good and strives to obtain it. The happy man, therefore, is he who can make the right judgment in all things."

The above quote from Seneca points to the importance of rationality and the elimination of emotions when making judgments. Making a judgment with a disturbed mind would not likely be the best decision when we start reviewing after becoming sober. When the mind is filled with raging emotions, it makes bad decisions along that line.

Imagine making a decision or executing an action right after you just lost your job. The first thing that comes to your mind definitely won't be something positive, as you will go completely blank and your mind far away from reality. It will take the grace of God for one not to do anything stupid. That is the power irrationality holds over us when our mind is clouded.

However, a Stoic will maintain an indifferent stand irrespective of the magnitude of the situation. Not because they don't care. Not because they don't feel pains or pleasures. But because their minds have been trained stoically to be indifferent to any feeling whatsoever. That is the attribute of a true Stoic.

Upholding virtue ahead of immorality also helps in attaining happiness. Been good and exuding virtues are key attributes of a Stoic. Do you really want to be happy? How about you start with this? This is the same thing that had worked for the likes of Marcus Aurelius, Seneca, and Epictetus.

When talking about the importance of virtue, Seneca argues, "What! Does virtue alone suffice to make you happy? Why? Of course, consummate and God-like virtue such as this not only suffices but more than suffices: for when a man is placed beyond the reach of any desire, what can he possibly lack? If all that he needs is concentered in himself, how can he require anything from without? It is that some are tied more or less tightly by these bonds, and some have even tied themselves with them as well; whereas he who has made progress towards the upper regions and raised himself upwards drags a looser chain, and though not yet free, is yet as good as free."

Virtue is everything. Virtue comes with good luck. However, there might be a time when one doesn't even tread the path of virtue and everything will still work in his or her favor. Technically, it might be attributed to mere luck and fortune that follows that person. Which is true. But, one who follows virtue is sure to reap goodness and happiness.

This long quote should tell you the importance of virtue as a principle of Stoicism. With that being said, how about you start wearing your best smile, answering rude or aggressive gestures with a warm smile or calm nod, and being good to all including yourself? That is the only way you can be truly happy and reach the stage of eudemonia.

As we are reaching the ending of this book, we would like to ask if it is becoming boring or getting more interesting? Well, you haven't seen anything yet as we would discuss even more on knowing what to control, what not to control, and how to know the difference in our next chapter.

Chapter Fourteen

After the Storm, Comes Peace

Now that you've learned all that is there to know about Stoicism, we are sure that your mind must understand the principles and tenets. Applying it to achieve peace and genuine happiness is the only step left for you to take. Most times, life presents us with more than what we can truly handle. Instead of giving up, we should learn to cultivate the habit of fighting through it, no matter the circumstances.

Having an in-depth knowledge about Stoicism paves the way for a clearer mind. As a matter of fact, true peace comes when we accept our pain. When we use our pain to forge ahead and create a new path for ourselves, that is true Stoicism.

No one likes pain. In fact, we all try to avoid passing through this phase, by all means necessary, even if it means cutting corners. But, pain is part of our life. It can strengthen our journey and give us a whole meaning to life. It can bring you closer to reality. Pain brings focus and in the long run reveals our true self. However, how to deal with our pain determines how we are turning out to be after the phase ends. Are you going to let your pain beat you up, or stay strong until it subsides?

Stoicism paves the way for us to realize how perfect and great being good will suit us, if only we will try. It shows us the easiest and cheapest path toward living a happy life, especially in line with virtue, rationality, and a perfectly maintained mental state. No one is truly living unless he or she holds nature high and conforms to its laws. Live your life in this manner and watch yourself grow.

The storm isn't over until you've learned to master and know yourself better. Marcus Aurelius didn't become famous for just sitting idle and ordering guards around. He was tactful, intelligent, and ready to see the brighter side of things no matter how sour they got.

To begin with, learn to successfully tweak and configure the way you think in an appropriate manner that will benefit you in the long run. Even Epictetus succumbs to this as he gives the two mitigating principles that guide how we end up or should actually control the things around us.

He agreed that we can control some things that happen around us. We can actually influence them into coming out in our favor. While, on the other hand, some are just completely out of our reach. They are controlled by nature and will end up influencing our lives. Thus, we end up getting unhappy by thinking too much of what we can't control. We even go extra length, thereby creating unnecessary stress for ourselves.

Epictetus continued with his argument by laying emphasis on what we cannot control. As a matter of fact, what we control is very little in comparison to what we can't seem to control. For example, we certainly can control nature. We also can't control how nature would pin its web around us. We can't control people's feelings about us. We can't force them to like us or hate us. Thus, what we can control is ourselves, and our thoughts, which influence our judgments and decisions.

Little wonder why we get mad if things don't go our way, especially we've put in lots of effort. But as the true Stoic we hope to become, shit happens. We now begin to see things around us as a combination of disappointment. Like they aren't working in our favor no matter how hard we try. These are nothing but just figments of our own imagination. They are things we create so as to give ourselves a much-needed excuse when things go south.

When we make wrong judgments about things around us, we should know that whatever deduction or conclusion we must have reached about a particular thing in our lives, it is bound to be different from what others feel about that particular thing. What you consider perfect might be full of blemish to another.

All these are called value judgments. And they are

one of the few things we have control over. Even if Stoicism pushes us to start thinking we have no control over everything in our lives (which is very true), it still points out happiness as one thing we have total control over. We have a right to be happy – truly happy. Even Epictetus agrees with this fact.

Secondly, your mind is your sanctuary, so train it perfectly, to withhold any condition. Stoicism agrees to the fact that life is hard, thus trying to train your mind while facing the world can be quite difficult. For example, it will be very difficult for someone who is putting himself through school and still trying to maintain a perfect mind. However, if one can achieve this feat, even while battling with everyday problems, then one is said to have attain the position of a true Stoic.

Also, take the life of Seneca as a guiding lesson. Seneca was rushed by a series of trial and obstacles. He was disgraced, exiled, lost lots of people that were dear to him, suffered as a slave, and was made to end his life by Nero. And when he knew it wasn't easy for anyone to follow virtue and goodness even in those situations, he stood his ground.

To this effect, Stoicism has made things easy for people that want to incorporate the principles in their daily lives. According to Stoicism pioneers, Marcus Aurelius and Seneca, it is easier said than done when following the core tenets of Stoicism. It is far bigger than just following the daily routines of your life.

Seneca had advised that in order to successfully incorporate and practice Stoicism in our daily lives, we should learn to start taking stock at the end of each day that passes. That way, you can jot down things that you don't even notice about yourself. You will be able to reflect on your mistakes and errors, becoming a better version of your self. For example, if you flare up unnecessarily at your subordinate, taking stock would make you assess that situation again and know if you are wrong.

Another way of incorporating Stoicism within our daily lives is one of the strategies used by the former Roman Emperor, Marcus Aurelius. Every morning, he would look up to himself and remind himself over and over again that no matter how hard he tried, he was bound to encounter difficult, stressed, ungrateful, impatient, annoying, and recalcitrant people every day of his life.

Therefore, this reflection he kept going through in advance would refresh his sense of reasoning and give him the patience he needed. He also acknowledged the fact that it is no fault of these people as they were also facing problems of their own. These problems were affecting them because of the way and manner in which their emotions ended up influencing their judgment.

Lastly, irrespective of how hard you think you might want to or try to influence nature, it's still going to be what it ought to be. In other words, accept nature and fate as your destiny. Accept the fact that if it is destined to be, then it will surely be. The world is way bigger than just our tiny little lives. Thus, we shouldn't hope to be the master of nature. Instead, we must accept whatever it throws in our way.

Expectations hurt in the long run, especially when we have put in too much hope. If we keep thinking "I pray it comes through," then it will never come through. But when we leave everything in the hands of nature, we do our best and leave the rest with the mindset of what will be, will be. We are indirectly preparing for the worst, which is a good sign for Stoicism.

Epictetus said, "If you expect the universe to deliver what you want, you are going to be disappointed, but if you embrace whatever the universe gives, then life will be a whole lot smoother."

Like we said earlier, this is just a piece of advice. But it is important to know that this advice is becoming relevant in today's world with lots of people trying to incorporate Stoicism within their daily lives.

Be that as it may, the storm will finally be over

when stability and peace come into your life. Knowing the difference between what you can control and what you can't is the pathway toward peace. Now, guess what? Things will now start taking shape. You would be amazed at the way things will move from good to better.

A lot of us miss out on this bumper offer Stoicism offers us. When we hear the word Stoicism, many of us don't even know what it's all about. Our ignorance is really making us miss out on all the goodness this philosophy comes with. The previous chapters of this book must have laid emphasis on the freebies that are attached to Stoicism.

Nothing gives peace better than having control. Trust me - you will have peace of mind knowing that everything that surrounds you is under your control. In our everyday life, it has to do with one thing in general, one that encompasses every other thing; shifting focus from the end result, or things to the achievements that resides inside them. Instead of focusing on how good or bad our decisions are, we should focus on what they have achieved. That's the only thing that will keep us going.

For example, if you are putting together a catchy resume for a job promotion at your place of work, then you need to set your goals right. Focusing on the outcomes would not be advisable. There is a 50:50

chance that you might not get the job. This is because the outcomes aren't in your control. However, you can choose to influence it - which still doesn't give you a hundred percent guarantee.

The best you can do is think of what you might want to achieve after bagging the job - the milestones you'd want to reach. This will give you the boost you need in writing a good resume. It is the Stoic way of doing things. Prepare your mind for both positive and negative outcomes, too.

Having control is the peace you deserve. It is far deeper than it sounds. The dichotomy of control has countless applications to everyday life, and all of them have to do with one crucial move; shifting your goals from external outcomes to internal achievements.

This will enable you to free yourself from any form of guilt or disappointment. It will give you peace of mind without any worries whatsoever. It is important to know that things don't always go the way we want. It's the wisest thing to do because even after we don't get the job, the best we can do is to forge ahead with our lives.

Shifting our focus from outcomes to achievements can help us keep some things in our lives under our control. That way, you will only focus on yourself with nobody to rival with at all. The only thing you will be competing with is making yourself a better version of what you were yesterday. Do this and you can be sure to enjoy nothing but a happy and serene life. Looking inwardly has also helped a lot of Stoics in keeping things under their control even when it seemed they were losing out.

Knowing what you control and what you don't is really not enough in getting the peace you deserve. Sometimes it takes much more than that to live a life of actual eudemonia. Mind you, the storm might be quite crazy to deal with in the beginning. Imagine someone going through a triple set back all at one time.

Let's say you lost a huge sum of money, your favorite pet ate poison behind you, and you lost your relationship with your boyfriend all at the same time. Now, that is one hell of a setback. Even the hardest of hearts between us would still melt at such a situation. However, after passing through the learnings of Stoicism, one would be surprised at how great you'd feel even after experiencing such a setback.

I know you must be feeling bad as we are reaching the last chapter of this book. I'm also sure you would agree with me that it been one hell of a ride since you started reading through this interesting book. Read through the next chapter as we put a lid on the top of our bottle of knowledge.

Chapter Fifteen

A New Dawn!

After the smooth ride, we've had together on the course of this book, I'm sure you would agree with me that something has changed in you – your perception toward living your life. There will be an urge for you to push yourself even further in achieving the goals you've set out for yourself. And remember - giving up is not an option.

Nothing like that exists in the Stoic dictionary. Immerse yourself with the kind of contentment and happiness Stoicism is going to bring you. According to many devoted Stoics, the new dawn that comes with practicing Stoicism is liberating and scintillating. Nothing beats that feeling of being free from unnecessary worry and serious emotions.

You now have your life in your hands. There is nothing anyone can say or do to intimidate you. Even if they try, they will eventually get tired and leave you alone. When you constantly start smiling over any tantrum they throw at you, when you start smiling at even their deepest taunts and tease, they will definitely back down.

Achieving this stage is not a day's job. At first, it might not look like your efforts are holding substance.

But do not give up. The world today holds lots of temptations and events that may trigger our inner feelings into manifesting even when we never summoned them. For example, after reading a book on Stoicism and really wanting to practice the principles in our daily lives, you start getting tempted to break your resolve with something that is totally out of your control.

Being an alcoholic or womanizer could be a very hard thing to control. Irrespective of how hard we try, sometimes our inner feelings toward these vanities of life may end up overcoming our mind, body, and soul entirely. Imagine an alcoholic asked not to taste even a pint for a week; quite crazy, right? Or a womanizer tempted with a very beautiful woman and expected to look the other way.

It takes more than just a resolution on our part. We must be ready to let go of every urge to the vanities of this world. Let's adopt the mind of everything is given to us by nature and can be taken away by nature. Seneca cultivated this mindset towards living his life as a slave and nature eventually came through for him.

Let's learn to start expecting less from people around us. We should never forget that no one is perfect or even has total control of the things around them. One way or the other, we are all different parts of the same cosmos. Our everyday activities in life are a contribution to a much bigger world. Whether we do good or bad, it all has its own effect on nature.

Being a Stoic now makes one thing very clear; everything happens for a reason. If you don't believe that, then I urge you to start believing. Nothing happens on its own without the influence of another. If you are rich today, it's obviously because you've put in much hard work in order to turn out successful. Also, if you are a prominent and skillful footballer loved by all, it's because you have also put in much hard work while training in order to come out on top.

There is a light at the end of the tunnel for everyone willing to start a brand new life with Stoicism. Try it for a week and watch your world go smoothly. If you are depressed before, Stoicism is the fastest solution you can think of. The present-day settings of the world have made Stoicism relevant to the daily struggles of life. People now become stressed at work. The unemployed become depressed at home. Couples and relationships become strained. Lots of people end up losing focus and direction.

Living the life of a Stoic is not an easy path. Though it will build up one's lost confidence and self-esteem, it will make you feel different from the rest. For example, would you rather save up or buy steak every weekend? Would you rather visit your loved ones or go on a walk? Questions like these are hard to answer when you live like a Stoic. And of course, Stoicism entails making an emotionless decision. Thus, how do you tell if you are being influenced?

Stoicism might tidy up one's life, but it does leave some dots behind. But one thing it doesn't forget to do is give us contentment in the decisions we make. Believe me, if we stop thinking about death and just focus on our lives and making them better, we will move even mountains. We will surpass every obstacle like it's nothing. The only way to lead a good life is to train your mind perfectly.

That aside, you will now start becoming aware of your environment. You will also start paying attention to the things you control and the ones that are out of your league. This is very important to because it will hold the key to your new world. Let's take this example, no matter low our income or occupation may be, so long we are within the age bracket of 24-30, we might want to start doing things to live healthily and keep fit.

We might go to the gym to build our muscles. We might even go take a walk around the park to clear out head each time we feel stuffed. Do a little bit of yoga and meditate until our problems finally dissolve away. We do this not because we want to look good for the girls. Neither are we doing it just to attract attention from work or even accomplish our set out objectives. Instead, we are doing it for ourselves. Because we want to fulfill our urge toward leading a fulfilling life, irrespective of what anyone thinks.

That is an action of a true Stoic. Do not let the actions of others put you off. Do not let their actions control you. And do not let their actions influence your decisions and judgments. A true Stoic configures his or her mind to be indifferent from whatever feelings that may erupt inside.

Be that as it may, it is widely known that Stoics all over the world tend to attribute the qualities of a God to their founding fathers. They see them as an epitome of perfection, forgetting that they were also mere mortals like the rest of us. Marcus Aurelius, Seneca, and Epictetus were mere mortals that made mistakes, lived among people, loved and were loved by people, and in fact, they lost also like every other mortal.

Their attributes can be likened to our moments in life. The same way we have behaved in the course of our life is how they behaved. They'd shed tears when hurt. They'd cried when pained. They'd smiled when happy. The list is endless. Thus, they are very wrong in that assumption.

We are far from perfect. We also make mistakes, but one thing we can surely do is to walk our way through and make corrections to being a better version of ourselves. That and more are the reason why Stoicism came into being. However, the beginning of

Stoicism wasn't to better mankind as a whole. It was actually a combination of their conversations, letters, medications, maxims, plays, diaries, and even notable events in their lives.

In moments of grief, they made sure they nursed themselves with their writings of strong will. In moments of obstacles and problems, they meditated their way through. They continuously tried making themselves better and better every day that passed in their lives. Therefore, can't we just be like that?

Why can't we strive hard and build ourselves back up each time we are down? Why can't we look up each time we are facing what may seem to be bigger and stronger than us? Why can't we soulfully meditate through our problems instead of sticking to alcohol and other social vices?

With that being said, practicing Stoicism perfectly doesn't need one to be a Ph.D. holder. As a matter of fact, there is little or no need for one to start writing crazy essays and books all in the name of practicing it. It is far from citing up words from the sayings of the early Stoics just to feel cool. It should be imbibed in our life.

It is also not a religion, it has no tenets that are grounded on the basis of religion. But it opens up our eyes to the possibility of living a life of absolute importance. This tenet had been upgraded and modernized from generation to generation. It had passed through reformation and transformation.

In the 20th century, there was low acceptance of the philosophy, but the 21st century gave rise to a whole new perspective as the philosophy gained popularity and recognition with lots of people applying it in their lives. To this effect, Modern Stoics have managed to tweak the principles so as to fit the settings of the modern world. And these tweaked principles make it more acceptable for people to enjoy and embrace the philosophy.

It has helped lots of people in finding a permanent solution to their problems. For example, let's say your friend had gone through one of the craziest and sensitive stage in his or her life. Imagine someone going through a double hurt. Losing a job and also losing one's parent (mum or dad) can be quite crazy. At that particular point in time, it will take every nerve in someone to hold his or her sanity.

Your friend would definitely not be the same again. Something must have changed in him or her. Something must have been broken in him or her. What can help is Stoicism. Stoicism will give that person a sense of reasoning. Stoicism will provide the strength to look the other way and carry on with his or her life. Stoicism will ensure you become strong - stronger than you can even imagine. It will teach you how to be good and see the world from a different perspective, thereby becoming happy.

Living in the new dawn of your life entails a few things and they are as follows;

1. **Eliminating Emotions:** This is something you must be familiar with at this point in time. It is one of the core principles of being a Stoic. If we can cultivate a mind where emotions can be overlooked, then we can proudly say that we have reached a stage of being a Stoic, thereby reaching eudemonia.

    Learn to control the mind. Learn to know what you can control and what you can not. Know the distinction between these two and everything will start working in your favor. When we feel angry about something that seems to be out of our control, we are only allowing these things or people get to us.

    However, we will also reach a point in the time of our lives where getting angry will be useless and unnecessary. In situations where anger used to be our only resolve, we will now start getting calm. This is when we've reached true Stoicism. Thus, the new dawn Stoicism will bring to our lives will be immense happiness and freedom from stress.

2. **Learn and Practice:** Learning is an everyday process. As the saying goes, no one knows it all.

Thus, we strive to become better, every day of our life. Pick up a book or two about Stoicism. Ensure you immerse yourself completely in the teachings and lessons. They might come in handy when solving a problem or two.

Don't get it twisted, learning is a continuous process. The same thing goes for Stoicism. As the world we live in today keeps changing continuously, the scholars of Stoicism keep reforming and making great changes to the principles of this philosophy so as to suit our world. Now, immerse yourself with the current state of things. Always know if there is any change. This can only be achieved when we keep learning every day.

Instead of staying glued and attached to just a particular type of information about Stoicism, why not get yourself immersed and updated with new formulations, knowledge, and scholarly ideas of Modern Stoics? These may come in different languages and training. To know is to forget and to practice is to remember.

3. **Accept Nature:** According to science, nature is orderly and regular. It is very organized and surrounds us with its beauty and mystery. Stoicism acknowledges the presence and supremacy of nature over us. Man and nature have a relationship which makes both of them

connected, yet distinctive.

As Marcus Aurelius puts it when complimenting this perspective, "At every moment keep a sturdy mind on the task at hand, as a Roman and human being, doing it with strict and simple dignity, affection, freedom, and justice—giving you a break from all other considerations. You can do this if you approach each task as if it is your last, giving up every distraction, emotional subversion of reason, and all drama, vanity, and complaint about your fair share. You can see how mastery over a few things makes it possible to live an abundant and devout life—for, if you keep watch over these things, the gods won't ask for more."

4. **Living with Death in Your Heart:** We will all die someday. This perception will keep you on your toes. It will make you start thinking of how best to live your life. If you are always attending funeral services (we are not saying you should start attending funeral services), you would learn to understand and appreciate the true meaning of life.

Why waste your life doing things that won't give you the fulfilment you seek? Early Stoics have laid emphasis on this subject matter. This will show you that even those Roman thinkers always had it at the back of their minds that death is just a stone's throw away, thus, gearing them towards living a great life.

"Memento mori" is the mantra of all Stoics, thereby making them take the issue of death seriously. Thinking about death would make them remain focused on the principles and tenets to the philosophy.

But today, many people don't even want to spare a second thought for death. They obviously know that they will surely due someday, but they just don't want to picture themselves dying. Therefore, they end up spending large hospital bills, buying long life medicines, visiting Shamans, and even going on a meditation trip all in an attempt at prolonged life. Meanwhile, their focus should be living a good and happy life for the time being.

5. **Know Thyself (Erecting an Inner Citadel):** We have raised emphasis on this part of Stoicism in the previous chapters. This is the first step to practicing Stoicism - the first thing to do when your mind is made up about following the path of Stoicism. We know our true self. No one knows us better than ourselves.

People can only get to us when we allow them in; when we show them the way to our mind. That is when they will spin their web of controversies and influence our decisions and judgments. We will be powerless as we will keep watching them without being able to raise a finger.

This is where looking inward and trusting yourself, knowing what you really want, is important, what you are really made of, and what you really seek in life. Build a formidable inner fortress that can not be penetrated no matter how much every variable working against you tries.

For instance, a man who had survived from a region where war, destruction, famine, and hunger dictates the days of his life would have developed a strong inner citadel which will be capable of holding him through any moment of his life. With the amount of chaos he faced, he had been able to look inward for a solution, thereby, becoming resolute, resonant, and totally indifferent from pain or pleasure.

Be that as it may, this brings us to the end of our esteemed book on Stoicism as a pathway to achieving complete happiness and peace. We will implore you to follow this path with much importance. This new dawn in your life is an opportunity for you to live your life appropriately. It is a second chance many don't even get at all.

Live well, stay happy, uphold virtue, and never allow your emotions to make the better part of your decisions and judgments. Do all this and you will be fine.

Conclusion

I'm afraid this is the end of this amazing and educational book which we believe had opened your eyes to the principles of Stoicism and its application to achieving complete happiness. I'm sure you would agree with me that Stoicism is one hell of a philosophy. Hard to maintain but very effective when applied.

And if you can maintain its application in your daily life, nothing can stop you from achieving all that you have set out to – well, except death, of course. This book has given you a new path to seek toward achieving what you feel is unachievable. Follow and tread the path steadily until it takes you to where your destination – eudemonia.

But rest assured, your perception of the world has changed. A lot of your buddies might start asking questions like, "what's happening, mate? Why the sudden change? Are you alright?" Such questions are bound to come, especially when you start applying what this book had taught you about Stoicism – eliminating emotions, being logical always, upholding virtue, and so much more. Do not let their comments deter you. In fact, if they conclude on parting ways with you, then so be it. They are obviously not the right circle you should be in.

The chapters of this book are outlined in a step-by-step format which should help you in understanding the philosophy of Stoicism even better. With lots of examples and real-life situations, we can refer back to it whenever we are facing or passing through a rough phase in our lives.

Never give up the fight toward being a better version of yourself. Continue to strive hard, the way Seneca and Marcus Aurelius, did even in tribulations. Immerse yourself with your situation. Accept it, whether good or bad. That is the only way you can move past it.

What you've gained from this book is a knowledge that can never be bought. Use it well, and help share with others if you can. You can even become a help to someone who needs it. Not everyone passing through a rough phase would want to voice out. Reach out to them and use Stoicism to heal them the way Seneca healed Lucilius.

And this brings us to the end. But, guess what? It's the beginning of a new dawn for you. As you are closing this book, you are opening the beginning of a new life with a fresh path. So the question remains, what are you going to do with this new light in your life? Throw it away? Or follow it until it fades?

Enjoy every day this new path brings forth. Live your life stoically like it's your last day as you apply the tips and ideas this book has offered you. And always remember, even when the enjoyment of living like a Stoic didn't immediately start manifesting, giving up is never an option for true Stoics. Thank you for sticking with us this far.

Good luck and God bless!

***

www.ingramcontent.com/pod-product-compliance
Lightning Source LLC
Chambersburg PA
CBHW070952080526
44587CB00015B/2269